D1329326

The Three Battlegrounds

Francis Frangipane

New Wine Press

British edition

New Wine Press
PO Box 17
Chichester
West Sussex PO20 6YB
England

Copyright © 1994 Francis Frangipane

All rights reserved. No part of this publication may be reproduced,
stored in a retrieval system, or transmitted in any form or by any
means, electronic, mechanical, photocopying, recording or
otherwise.

Short extracts may be used for review purposes.

Unless otherwise stated all Scripture quotations are from the New
American Standard Bible. © 1960, 1962, 1963, 1968, 1971, 1972,
1973, 1975, 1977 The Lockman Foundation, La Habra, California.
Used by permission.
KJ – King James version, Crown copyright.
Amplified – Scripture taken from The Amplified Bible, Old
Testament copyright © 1965, 1987 by The Zondervan Corporation.
The Amplified New Testament copyright © 1958, 1987 by
The Lockman Foundation. Used by permission.

ISBN: 1 874367 26 4

Copies of some of these messages are available on audio cassette
and can be purchased by writing to: River of Life Ministries,
PO Box 10102, Cedar Rapids, IA 52410, USA.

Also available by this author and published by New Wine Press:

In the Presence of God – A powerful and penetrating study of the
human heart and how God prepares it for His glory. (Previously
published under the title *Holiness, Truth and the Presence of God*.)

Typeset by CRB (Drayton) Typesetting Services, Drayton, Norwich
Printed in England by Clays Ltd, St Ives plc.

Acknowledgements

Special thanks to ...

Allen Bond, Marilyn Bryant, Kevin Dwyer, Erma Lam, Lila Nelson and Orv Schinke for their many hours of editing, their patience and sacrifice in putting this work together.

I also want to especially thank my wife, Denise, and our five children, who lovingly and patiently gave of themselves that I might finish this task.

Most importantly, we each want to thank the Lord Jesus, for His continued grace and faithfulness in guiding this work to its conclusion.

Contents

Contents

Preface

We would encourage our readers to become familiar with the glossary in the back of this book. Also, from time to time we update our text. If you see some things differently than we do, please let us know. As the Lord leads, we will make necessary revisions in a subsequent printing.

No one is more mindful of the fact that we are exploring uncharted regions of a subject that is ever unfolding. There is yet much wisdom and knowledge to discover in these dimensions. Therefore, let us approach these studies being mindful of our present inadequacies.

At the same time, this volume will serve as a companion for those serious prayer warriors and leaders who are making preparations for the days ahead. As we pass to you our information, our confidence is that the Lord Himself has set His heart to guide us. In Him, all things are complete; and by relying upon Him, all things become adequate.

Introduction

This is a book about spiritual warfare. Before we proceed, however, I have two concerns. The first is our need for wisdom. There is an old European proverb worth heeding. It reads:

'Age and treachery will always defeat youth and zeal.'

Before we engage in spiritual warfare, we should know this about Satan: He is an ancient and extremely treacherous foe. On the other hand, the strength of most Christians lies primarily in idealism and untested fervour. It is not long, usually five to ten years in the ministry, and most zeal has waned. Without warning, the minister's call has deteriorated from a walk of vision to a mere job.

What occurred was that zeal, by itself, challenged the treachery of hell and lost. The brightness of youthful dreams dimmed under the dark cloud of relentless satanic assault. Under the weight of growing frustrations and discouragement, compromise increased, and with it came iniquity and spiritual bondage.

Yet, the real villain was not sin, but ignorance. We put the devil in a doctrinal box and expected him to stay there. He did not. He undermined relationships, and our love grew cautious. He resisted us in prayer, and our faith turned weak. Disillusionment set in. After spending much time with struggling pastors, I have seen a common trend in most: **They failed to discern the assault of the devil**. They stood unprotected against an ancient and treacherous foe.

Jesus prepared His disciples for everything, including war. They saw Him casting out demons. In fact, He sent them forth doing the same. But before He sent them out, He charged them to become wise *'as serpents'* yet innocent and harmless *'as doves'* (Matthew 10:16). This fusion of divine **wisdom** and Christlike **innocence** is the taproot of all spiritual victory. Indeed, we can defeat the enemy, but wisdom must precede warfare and virtue must come before victory.

Consequently, the goal of this book is to train the church in wisdom and call the church to innocence. We will not disregard what we have previously learned; we will still **live** by faith. But we must learn the ways of God, which means we must **think** with wisdom. And we must be pure of heart, that we may see God and gain discernment. Indeed, it is this very ignorance that has left us vulnerable to satanic attack.

Of my second concern, let me say that there are no shortcuts to successful warfare; only ways to make it longer and more perilous. One way of peril is to enter battle blinded by presumption. When it comes to waging war effectively, consider carefulness to be the essence of victory.

Whatever lofty spiritual plane you imagine that you are on, remember, Adam was in **Paradise** when he fell. Before your increased knowledge and religious experiences make you overly self-confident, recall that Solomon wrote three books of Scripture, **he actually gazed upon the glory of God**, yet he fell. Yes, even in your deepest worship of the Almighty do not forget, in long ages past **Lucifer himself was once in Heaven**, pouring out praise to God.

We all have seen many who have fallen. Jesus warned that the love of many would grow cold. Do not presume it cannot happen to you. Our enemy has been deceiving mankind for thousands of years. Our experience, on the other hand, spans but a brief moment. It is wisdom to recognize that we do not know all there is to know concerning warfare.

Therefore, be bold, but never brash or arrogant in your prayer life. Use your spiritual authority administratively, compassionately, but never presumptuously. Multitudes of well-meaning but ignorant Christians have approached the field of spiritual battle with flippant attitudes and have suffered greatly for it. Study several books and seek confirmation from the Lord for your strategies. As it is written,

> *'Prepare plans by consultation, and make war by wise guidance.'* (Proverbs 20:18)

Thus, our purpose here is to help equip you for battle in each of the three primary battlegrounds: the mind, the church and the heavenly places. There certainly are other fields or subcategories of spiritual warfare; however, these are where most of us will face conflict.

One last note. A few of you will be instrumental in actually saving your cities. Our prayer is that these chapters will help guide and equip you for that goal. The promise of the Spirit speaks thus:

> *'There was a small city with few men in it and a great king came to it, surrounded it, and constructed large siege-works against it. But there was found in it a poor wise man and he delivered the city by his wisdom.'* (Ecclesiastes 9:14–17)

While many are predicting the destruction of our nation and the collapse of our cities, they have not considered the power of **Christ in you**. But remember,

> *'Wisdom is better than strength ... wisdom is better than weapons of war.'* (Ecclesiastes 9:16, 18)

Francis Frangipane
July 1989

PART ONE:

The Battleground of the Mind

You will remember that the location where Jesus was crucified was called 'Golgotha', which meant 'place of the skull'. If we will be effective in spiritual warfare, the first field of conflict where we must learn warfare is the battleground of the mind; i.e., the 'place of the skull'. For the territory of the uncrucified thought-life is the beachhead of satanic assault in our lives. To defeat the devil, we must be crucified in the place of the skull. We must be renewed in the spirit of our minds!

Chapter 1

Satan's Domain:
The Realm of Darkness

Many Christians debate whether the devil is on the earth or in hell; can he dwell in Christians or only in the world? The fact is, the devil is in darkness. Wherever there is spiritual darkness, there the devil will be.

Preparing for Spiritual Warfare

For most, the term 'spiritual warfare' introduces a new, but not necessarily welcomed, dimension in their Christian experience. The thought of facing evil spirits in battle is an unsettling concept, especially since we came to Jesus as lost sheep, not warriors. Ultimately, some of us may never actually initiate spiritual warfare, but all of us must face the fact that the devil has initiated warfare against us. Therefore, it is essential to our basic well-being that we discern the areas of our nature which are unguarded and open to satanic assault.

Jude tells us,

> *'And angels who did not keep their own domain, but abandoned their proper abode, He has kept in eternal bonds under darkness for the judgment of the great day.'* (Jude vs 6).

When Satan rebelled against God, he was placed under eternal judgment in what the Bible calls 'pits' or 'bonds' of

15

darkness. The devil, and the fallen angels with him, have been relegated to live in darkness. This darkness does not simply mean 'lightless regions' or areas void of visible light. The eternal darkness to which this Scripture refers is essentially a **moral** darkness, which does ultimately degenerate to literal darkness. However, its cause is not simply the absence of light; it is the absence of God, Who is light.

It is vital to recognize that this darkness to which Satan has been banished is not limited to areas outside of humanity. Unlike those who do not know Jesus, however, we have been delivered out of the domain or 'authority' of darkness (Colossians 1:13). We are not trapped in darkness if we have been born of Light. But if we **tolerate** darkness through tolerance of sin, we leave ourselves vulnerable for satanic assault. For wherever there is wilful disobedience to the Word of God, there is spiritual darkness and the potential for demonic activity.

Thus Jesus warned, *'Take heed, that the light which is in you be not in darkness'* (Luke 11:35 KJ). There is a light in you. *'The spirit of man is the lamp of the Lord...'* (Proverbs 20:27). Your spirit, illuminated by the Spirit of Christ, becomes the 'lamp of the Lord' through which He searches your heart. There is indeed a holy radiance surrounding a true Spirit-filled Christian. But when you harbour sin, the *'light which is in you'* is *'in darkness.'* Satan has a legal access, given to him by God, to dwell in the domain of darkness. We must grasp this point: **The devil can traffic in any area of darkness, even the darkness that still exists in a Christian's heart**.

God's Thresher

An example of Satan having access to the carnal side of human nature is seen in Peter's denial of Jesus. It is obvious that Peter failed. What we do not readily see, however, is what was going on in the invisible world of the spirit.

Jesus predicted accurately that Peter would deny Him three times. Anyone looking at Peter's actions that night might have simply concluded his denial was a manifestation of fear. Yet, Peter was not fearful by nature. This was the disciple who, a few hours earlier, drew a sword against the multitudes who had come to arrest Jesus. No, human fear did not cause Peter to deny the Lord. Peter's denial was satanically induced.

Jesus had warned the apostle,

> *'Simon, Simon, behold, Satan has demanded per-mission to sift you like wheat; but I have prayed for you that your faith may not fail; and you, when once you have turned again, strengthen your brothers.'*
>
> (Luke 22:31–32)

Behind the scenes, Satan had demanded and received per-mission to sift Peter like wheat. Satan had access to an area of darkness in Peter's heart.

How did Satan cause Peter's fall? After eating the Pas-sover, Jesus told His disciples that one of them was going to betray Him. The Scripture then continues,

> *'And they began to discuss among themselves which one of them ... was going to do this thing.'*   (Luke 22:23)

This was a very sombre time. Yet, during this terrible moment we read,

> *'And there arose also a dispute among them as to which one of them was ... greatest.'*   (Luke 22:24)

They went from an attitude of shock and dismay to an argument concerning who among them was the greatest! Evidently Peter, the 'water-walker', who was also the boldest and most outspoken of the apostles, prevailed. We can imagine that Peter's high visibility among the disciples left him with an air of superiority, which was fanned by Satan into an attitude of presumption and boasting. Peter, being lifted up by pride, was being set up for a fall.

'*Pride*', the Scripture tells us, '*...cometh before a fall*' (Proverbs 16:18 KJ). Pride caused Satan's fall, and pride was the very same darkness Satan was using to cause Peter's fall. Lucifer, from experience, knew well the judgment of God against religious pride and envy. Satan did not have a right to indiscriminately assault and destroy Peter. He had to secure permission from Peter's Lord before he could come against the apostle. But the fact is, the devil demanded permission ... and he received it.

Submit to God

The trip-wire that Satan used to cause Peter's fall was the disciple's own sin of pride. **Let us recognize, before we do warfare, that the areas we hide in darkness are the very areas of our future defeat.** Often the battles we face will not cease until we discover and repent for the darkness that is within us. If we will be effective in spiritual warfare, we must be discerning of our own hearts; we must walk humbly with our God. Our first course of action must be '*Submit ... to God*'. Then, as we '*...resist the devil*', he will flee (James 4:7).

The good news, for Peter and ourselves, is that Satan will never be given permission to destroy the saints. Rather, he is limited to sifting them '*like wheat*'. There is wheat inside each of us. The outcome of this type of satanic assault, which is allowed through the permissive will of God, is to cleanse the soul of pride and produce greater meekness and transparency in our lives. It may feel terrible, but God causes it to work for good. Our husk-like outer nature must die to facilitate the breaking forth of the wheat-like nature of the new creation man. Both the chaff and the husk were necessary; they provided protection for us from the harsh elements of this life. But before God can truly use us, in one way or another, we will pass through a time of threshing.

Peter's husk nature was presumptuous and proud. His initial successes had made him ambitious and self-oriented.

God can never entrust His Kingdom to anyone who has not been broken of pride, for pride is the armour of darkness itself. So, when Satan demanded permission to assault Peter, Jesus said in effect, 'You can sift him, but you cannot destroy him.' The warfare against Peter was devastating, but measured. It served the purpose of God.

Peter was ignorant of the areas of darkness within him, and his ignorance left him open to attack. But the Lord would ask each of us, 'Do **you** know the areas where you are vulnerable to satanic assault?' Jesus would have us not be ignorant of our need. In fact, when He reveals the sin in our hearts, it is so He might destroy the works of the devil. We should realize that **the greatest defense we can have against the devil is to maintain an honest heart before God**.

When the Holy Spirit shows us an area that needs repentance, we must overcome the instinct to defend ourselves. We must silence the little lawyer who steps out from a dark closet in our minds, pleading, 'My client is not so bad.' Your 'defense attorney' will defend you until the day you die – and if you listen to him you will never see what is wrong in you, nor face what needs to change. For you to succeed in warfare, your self-preservation instincts must be submitted to the Lord Jesus; for Christ alone is your true advocate.

We cannot engage in spiritual battle without embracing this knowledge. Indeed, James 4:6 says,

> '. . . *God is opposed to the proud, but gives grace to the humble.*'

God is opposed to the proud. That is a very important verse. If God is opposed to the proud, and we are too proud to humble ourselves and admit we were wrong, **then God is opposed to us!**

James continues in verse 7,

> '*Submit therefore to God. Resist the devil and he will flee from you.*'

When we see this verse, it is usually all by itself as a monument to spiritual warfare. However, **it is in the context of repentance, humility and possessing a clean heart that we find Satan fleeing from us!**

We must go beyond a vague submission to God; we must submit the exact area of our personal battle to Him. When we come against the power of the devil, it must be from a heart in submission to Jesus.

There is a recurring precept throughout this book. It is vital that you know, understand and apply this principle for your future success in spiritual warfare. That principle is this:

> **Victory begins with the name of Jesus on your lips; but it will not be consummated until the nature of Jesus is in your heart.**

This rule applies to every facet of spiritual warfare. Indeed, Satan will be allowed to come against the area of your weakness until you realize God's only answer is to become Christlike. As you begin to appropriate not just the name of Jesus, but His nature as well, the adversary will withdraw. **Satan will not continue to assault you if the circumstances he designed to destroy you are now working to perfect you!**

The outcome of Peter's experience was that, after Pentecost, when God used him to heal a lame man, a new, humble Peter spoke to the gathering crowd.

> '...*Why do you gaze at us, as if by our own power or piety we had made him walk?*' (Acts 3:12b)

Peter's victory over pride and the devil began with the name of Jesus on his lips; and it was consummated by the nature of Jesus in his heart. The darkness in Peter was displaced with light, the pride in Peter was replaced with Christ.

Chapter 2

The Stronghold of the Godly: Humility

Satan fears virtue. He is terrified of humility; he hates it. He sees a humble person and it sends chills down his back. His hair stands up when Christians kneel down, for humility is the surrender of the soul to God. The devil trembles before the meek, because in the very areas where he once had access, there stands the Lord, and Satan is terrified of Jesus Christ.

Who Truly Are You Fighting?

You will remember that, at the fall of man in the Garden of Eden, the judgment of God against the devil was that he should *'eat dust'*. Remember also that God said of man, *'dust thou art'* (Genesis 3:14–19 KJ). The essence of our carnal nature – of all that is carnal in nature – is dust. We need to see the connection here: Satan feeds upon our earthly, carnal nature of *'dust'*. Satan dines on what we withhold from God.

Therefore, we need to recognize that the immediate source of many of our problems and oppressions is not demonic, but fleshly in nature. We must contend with the fact that one aspect of our lives, our flesh nature, will always be targeted by the devil. These fleshly areas supply Satan with a ready avenue of access to undermine our prayers and neutralize our walk with God.

It is only our exaggerated sense of self-righteousness that

prevents us from looking honestly at ourselves. We know Who is in us, but we must also know **what** is in us, if we will be successful in our war against the devil. Therefore, be specific when you submit yourself to God. Do not rationalize your sins and failures. **The sacrifice of Jesus Christ is a perfect shelter of grace enabling all men to look honestly at their needs.** Accordingly, be honest with God. He will not be horrified or shocked by your sins. God loved you without restraint even when sin was rampant within you; how much more will He continue to love you as you seek His grace to be free from iniquity?

Before we launch out in aggressive warfare, we must realize that many of our battles are merely the consequences of our own actions. To war effectively, we must separate what is of the flesh from what is of the devil.

Allow me to give you an example. My wife and I once lived in an area where a beautiful red cardinal kept its nest. Cardinals are very territorial and will fight off intruding cardinals zealously. At that time, we owned a van which had large side mirrors and chrome bumpers. Occasionally, the cardinal would attack the bumpers or mirrors, thinking his reflection was another bird. One day, as I watched the cardinal assail the mirror, I thought, 'What a foolish creature; his enemy is merely the reflection of himself.' Immediately the Lord spoke to my heart, **'And so also are many of your enemies the reflection of yourself.'**

Before we have any strategy for attacking Satan, we must make sure that the real enemy is not our own carnal nature. We must ask ourselves: are the things oppressing us today the harvest of what we planted yesterday?

Agree With Thine Adversary

You will remember that Jesus taught,

> *'Agree quickly with thine adversary, while you are on the way with him; lest at any time the adversary deliver thee to the judge, and the judge deliver thee to the*

officer, and thou be cast into prison. Verily I say unto thee, thou shalt by no means come out thence, till thou hast paid the uttermost farthing.'

(Matthew 5:25–26 KJ)

Jesus is speaking here of more than avoiding lawsuits. In fact, He speaks in such a way as to indicate that, in regards to this particular adversary and this particular judge, we will always lose our case and end up in prison.

This parable explains God's view of human righteousness. In the narrative, the adversary is the devil and the Judge is God. Satan, as our adversary, stands as the accuser of the brethren before God, the Judge of all. The truth Christ wants us to see is that when we approach God on the basis of our own righteousness, the adversary will always have legal grounds to *'cast* [us] *into prison,'* for our righteousness is *'... as filthy rags'* (Isaiah 64:6).

When Jesus says, *'agree quickly with thine adversary,'* He does not mean 'obey' the devil. He is saying that when Satan accuses you of some sin or flaw, if the devil is even minutely right, it is to your advantage to agree with him about your unrighteousness. If he accuses you of being impure, or not loving or praying enough, **he is right**. The key is not to argue with the devil about your own righteousness, because before God, your righteousness **is** unacceptable. No matter how much you defend or justify yourself, you know inwardly that often the accusations of the devil have morsels of truth in them.

Our salvation is not based upon what we do, but upon Who Jesus becomes to us. Christ Himself is our righteousness. We have been justified by faith; our peace with God comes through our Lord Jesus Christ (Romans 5:1). When Satan comes against you, he tries to deceive you by focusing your attention upon your own righteousness. The more we recognize that Jesus alone is our righteousness, the less the adversary can assault us in the arena of our failings.

When the accuser comes seeking to condemn you for not having enough love, your response should be, 'That is true,

I do not have enough love. But, the Son of God died for **all** my sins, even the sin of imperfect love.' Step out from the shadow of satanic assault and stand in the Brightness of your Father's love. Submit yourself to God and ask for Christ's love and forgiveness to replace your weak and imperfect love.

When Satan seeks to condemn you for impatience, again your response should be, 'Yes, in my flesh I am very impatient. But since I have been born again, **Jesus** is my righteousness and through His blood I am forgiven and cleansed.' Turn again to God. Use the accusation as a reminder that you are not standing before a throne of judgment, but rather a throne of grace which enables you to boldly draw near to God for help (Hebrews 4:16).

A vital key, therefore, to overcoming the devil is humility. To humble yourself is to refuse to defend your image: you **are** corrupt and full of sin in your old nature! Yet, we have a **new** nature which has been created in the likeness of Christ (Ephesians 4:24), so we can agree with our adversary about the condition of our flesh!

But do not limit this principle of humbling yourself only when you are involved in spiritual warfare. This precept is applicable in other situations as well. The strength of humility is that it builds a spiritual defense around your soul, prohibiting strife, competition and many of life's irritations from stealing your peace.

A wonderful place to practice this is in your family relationships. As a husband, your wife may criticize you for being insensitive. A fleshly response could easily escalate the conversation into a conflict. The alternative is to simply humble yourself and agree with your wife. You probably were insensitive. Then pray together and ask God for a more tender love.

As a wife, perhaps your husband accuses you of not understanding the pressures he has at work. More than likely he is right, you do not know the things he must face. Instead of responding with a counter-charge, humble yourself and agree with him. Pray together, asking God to give you an understanding heart. If we remain humble in heart, we will receive abundant grace from God and Satan will be disarmed on many fronts.

Remember, Satan fears virtue. He is terrified of humility; he hates it because humility is the surrender of the soul to the Lord, and the devil is terrified of Jesus Christ.

Chapter 3

Pulling Down Strongholds

What men call 'salvation' is simply the first stage of God's plan for our lives, which is to conform us in character and power to the image of Jesus Christ. If we fail to see our relationship to God as such, we will allow too many areas within us to remain unchanged. Pulling down strongholds is the demolition and removal of these old ways of thinking so that the actual Presence of Jesus Christ can be manifested through us.

What is a Stronghold?

> *'For though we walk in the flesh, we do not war according to the flesh, for the weapons of our warfare are not of the flesh, but divinely powerful for the pulling down of strongholds.'*   (2 Corinthians 10:3–5 KJ)

All successful deliverance must begin by first removing that which defends the enemy. In speaking of spiritual warfare, the Apostle Paul enlists the word 'stronghold' to define the spiritual fortresses wherein Satan and his legions hide and are protected. These fortresses exist in the **thought-patterns** and **ideas** that govern individuals and churches, as well as communities and nations. Before victory can be claimed, these strongholds must be pulled down and Satan's armour removed. Then the mighty weapons of the Word and the Spirit can effectively plunder Satan's house.

But what is the biblical meaning of this word, *'stronghold'*? In the Old Testament, a stronghold was a fortified dwelling used as a means of protection from an enemy. We find that David hid from King Saul in wilderness strongholds at Horesh (1 Samuel 23:14, 19). These were physical structures, usually caves high on a mountainside, and were very difficult to assault. It was with this imagery in mind that the inspired writers of the Bible adapted the word 'stronghold' to define powerful, vigorously protected spiritual realities.

A stronghold can be a source of protection for us from the devil, as is the case when the Lord becomes our stronghold (Psalm 18:2). Or conversely, a stronghold can be a source of defense for the devil, where demonic or sinful activity is actually defended within us by our sympathetic thoughts toward evil. The strongholds we are going to expose first are those wrong attitudes that protect and defend the old self-life, which very often become the 'fortified dwellings' of demonic oppression in a person's life.

The Apostle Paul defines a stronghold as

> *'...speculations,* [a] *lofty thing raised up against the knowledge of God.'*   (2 Corinthians 3:5)

A demonic stronghold is any type of thinking that exalts itself above the knowledge of God, thereby giving the devil a secure place of influence in an individual's thought-life.

In most cases, we are not talking about 'spirit-possession'. This author does not believe that a Christian can be possessed, for when a person is 'possessed' by a demon, that demon fills their spirit the way the Holy Spirit fills the spirit of a Christian.

However, Christians can be 'oppressed' by demons, which can occupy unregenerated thought-systems, especially if those thoughts are defended by self-deception or false doctrines! The thought, 'I cannot have a demon because I am a Christian,' is simply untrue. A demon cannot have you in an eternal, possessive sense, but **you can have a demon** if you refuse to repent of your sympathetic thoughts toward evil. Your rebellion toward God provides a place for the devil in your life.

A number of Christians are tormented by various fears. They have been counselled and prayed over, but to little avail. They needed more than prayer, they needed deliverance. But deliverance will probably be far from them until the **spirit of fear** is confronted and bound, and the stronghold of fear cast down.

Many believers have been taught that, because they have the Holy Spirit, they cannot be deceived. This also is untrue. One reason the Spirit of Truth was sent was because we so easily fall into self-deception. In fact, the very **thought** that a Christian cannot be deceived is itself a deception! Once that particular lie permeates a believer's mind, his ideas and opinions crystallize and remain in whatever state of spiritual immaturity he happens to be. All manner of spirits will attack the soul knowing they are protected by the armour of that person's own thoughts and doctrines!

It is quite difficult to break the power of religious self-deception, for the very nature of 'faith' is to give no room for doubt. Once a person is deceived, he does not recognize that he is deceived, because he has been deceived! For all that we think we know, we must know this as well: we can be wrong. If we refuse to accept this truth, how will we ever be corrected from our errors?

Any area of our heart or mind that is not surrendered to Jesus Christ is an area vulnerable to satanic attack. And it is here, uniquely in the uncrucified thought-life of the believer's mind, that the pulling down of strongholds is of vital importance. For this reason, we must attain what the Scriptures call 'humility of mind' before real deliverance is possible. When we discover rebellion toward God within us, we must not defend or excuse ourselves. Rather, we must humble our hearts and repent, exercising our faith in God to change us.

You see, Satan feeds upon sin. Wherever there is a habit of sin in a believer's life, expect to find demonic activity in that area. The sin-habit often becomes the dwelling place for a spirit that is robbing a believer of power and joy, and that habitation (or habit) is a stronghold.

You may not agree with the idea that evil spirits can frequent and occupy attitudes in a believer's life, but you must certainly agree that each of us has a carnal mind which is a source of vain imaginations and thoughts that exalt themselves above God (2 Corinthians 10:3–5). We deal with the devil by dealing with the carnal thought systems, the strongholds, that protect the enemy.

There were no strongholds, no wrong attitudes, no faulty thinking processes in Christ's mind. Just before Jesus went to His death, He remarked,

> '... *the ruler of this world cometh, but he has nothing in Me.*' (John 14:30)

Satan had nothing **in** Jesus. We also want to be able to say that Satan has no secret area inside us, no 'temptation-buzzer' he can push that will open the door of our soul toward evil. When the strongholds of our minds are toppled, though we may still occasionally fall into sin, we will walk in great victory. And we will be instrumental in helping others in their deliverance as well.

Repentance Precedes Deliverance

The pulling down of strongholds begins with repentance. When Jesus sent out His disciples,

> '*they went out and preached that men should repent. And they were casting out many demons ... and were healing.*' (Mark 6:12–13)

Regarding the deliverance of spirits that plague the mind, **repentance precedes deliverance, and deliverance often leads to healing in other areas**.

If you have been a Christian for any length of time, you have already had many strongholds broken in your life. These were broken when you repented and came to Jesus. Deliverance is often just that simple when a soul is willing. Yet, without some measure of repentance, deliverance is almost always impossible, for although a spirit may be commanded to leave, if the structure of the individual's thoughts has not been changed, his wrong attitude toward sin will welcome that spirit back.

One aspect of Christ's ministry is that '...*thoughts from many hearts may be revealed*' (Luke 2:35). If you will truly walk with Jesus, many areas of your thinking processes will be exposed. There will be a grace and a power from God to enable you to repent and believe God to impart His virtue into your life. You will see strongholds fall and victory come. But I must warn you, there will be pressure from your flesh, as well as from the demonic world itself, to minimize or ignore what God is requiring of you. You may be tempted to surrender just a token sin or some minor fault, while allowing your main problems to remain entrenched and well-hidden. Let us realize that the energies we expend in keeping our sins secret are the actual 'materials' of which a stronghold is made. The demon you are fighting is using **your** thoughts to protect his access to your life.

Let's pray:

> 'Heavenly Father, there are areas in my life (audibly name the habitual sins) that I have not fully surrendered to my Lord, Jesus Christ. Lord, forgive me of compromise. I also ask You for courage to approach the pulling down of strongholds without reluctance or wilful deception in my heart. By the power of the Holy Spirit and in the Name of Jesus, I bind the satanic influences that were reinforcing compromise and sin within me. I submit myself to the light of the Spirit of Truth to expose the strongholds of sin within me. By the mighty weapons of the Spirit and the Word, I

proclaim that each stronghold in my life is coming down! I purpose, by the grace of God, to have only one stronghold within me: the stronghold of the Presence of Christ!

I thank You, Lord, for forgiving and cleansing me from all my sins. And by the grace of God, I commit myself to follow through in this area until even the ruins of this stronghold are removed from my mind! Thank You, Father. In Jesus' name. Amen.'

Chapter 4

A House Made of Thoughts

There are satanic strongholds over countries and communities; there are strongholds which influence churches and individuals. Wherever a stronghold exists, it is a demonically-induced pattern of thinking. Specifically, it is a 'house made of thoughts' which has become a dwelling place for satanic activity.

A Warning Before Deliverance!

> *'Now when an unclean spirit goes out of a man, it passes through waterless places, seeking rest, and does not find it. Then it says, "I will return to my house from which I came."'*
> (Matthew 12:43–44)

Although the nature of an unclean spirit is, by definition, spiritual and not physical, it still seeks a dwelling place, a *'house'* where it may *'rest'*. Jesus revealed that there is a dimension to human nature that actually can host an evil spirit and provide it a type of rest. If that is so, let us expose the nature of man and uncover that aspect in us which can become the 'construction material' within which a spirit might lodge.

First let us realize that a demon cannot dwell in a true Christian's **spirit**. Through regeneration, the human spirit becomes the home of the Holy Spirit. Indeed, it is because the Holy Spirit is within us that we have discernment concerning the enemy's inroads.

The aspect of human nature which is most similar in substance and disposition to the nature of the evil one is the carnal thought-life, which is a dimension of the soul, or personality, of man. It is uniquely in our uncrucified thoughts and unsanctified attitudes that unclean spirits, masking themselves as **our** thoughts and hiding themselves in **our** attitudes, find access into our lives.

Jesus continued,

> '...*and when* [the unclean spirit] *comes, it finds* [its house] *unoccupied, swept, and put in order. Then it goes, and takes along with it seven other spirits more wicked than itself, and they go in and live there; and the last state of that man becomes worse than the first.*'
>
> (Matthew 12:44–45)

If you are going to be successful in spiritual battle, your warfare must be waged according to the Scriptures. For if you are ignorant of the necessity of bringing Christ into the delivered soul, there is the danger that the last state of '*that man*' might become '...*worse than the first*' (Matthew 12:45; 2 Peter 2:20). **Christ must enter and be allowed to build His house of righteousness in the very area where Satan once dwelt.** Except in cases of physical affliction, deliverance should not be attempted for anyone unwilling to submit their thought-life to Jesus Christ!

Removing Satan's Armour

> '*When a strong man fully armed guards his own homestead, his possessions are undisturbed; but when someone stronger than he attacks him and overpowers him, he takes away from him all his armor upon which he had relied, and distributes his plunder.*'
>
> (Luke 11:21–22)

Before we were saved, you and I were the 'undisturbed

possessions' of the devil; Satan was like a fully armed *'strong man'* guarding the homestead of our souls. On the day of our salvation, however, a glorious *'Someone stronger'*, the Lord Jesus Christ, attacked and overpowered Satan and stripped away his armour. Our born-again experiences may be widely varied on a natural level, but in the spirit-realm, a very similar war was waged and won for each of us. If we could have seen into the invisible world, we would have observed the Holy Spirit working with the angels of God to destroy the enemy's first line of defense, his *'armour'*. What exactly was this armour that protected the devil and kept us from salvation? The armour upon which demons rely consists of our own **thoughts**, **attitudes** and **opinions** which are in agreement with evil.

What Jesus described as *'armour'*, the apostle Paul classified as *'strongholds'* (2 Corinthians 10:1–4). It is important to recognize that, in speaking of strongholds, the apostle is addressing **the church**! It is foolish to assume that our salvation experience has eliminated all the wrong ideas and attitudes, the strongholds, which are still influencing our perceptions and behavior. Yes, old things passed away, and truly new things have come, but until we are walking in the fullness of Christ, we should not assume that the process of change is over.

We will be identifying some of these strongholds later in this chapter. For now, let us say that, on an individual level, the foundation of our continued success in warfare comes from yielding to the Lord as He reveals these strongholds, and agreeing with Him through repentance in pulling them down.

It is important to recognize that, when we speak of strongholds, we are not talking about random thoughts or occasional sins. Rather, the strongholds that affect us most are those which are so hidden in our thinking patterns that we do not recognize them nor identify them as evil. Remember, in our initial text, Jesus revealed that unclean spirits are seeking *'rest'*. The sense of rest they seek originates from being in harmony with their environment. In other words, when our thought-life is in agreement with unbelief, fear or habitual sin, the enemy has rest.

It is significant that the process of deliverance quite often involves a season of inner conflict and turmoil. This is a **good** sign, signifying the individual's will desires to be free. We should expect a time where we must exercise our authority in Christ as we *'resist'* the devil (1 Peter 5:9a). Paul speaks of the *'struggle'* of the church against principalities and powers. There will be a **period of fighting** involved in the process of pulling down strongholds, for you are breaking your agreement with a foe who will fight to remain in your life.

Taking Every Thought Captive to Christ

While we may find comfort in being Christians, being a Christian has not made us perfect. There are still many strongholds within us. Therefore, let us identify some of these spiritual fortresses. Rare is the Christian who is not limited by at least one of the following strongholds: unbelief, cold love, fear, pride, unforgiveness, lust, greed or any combination of these, as well as the possibility of many others.

Because we excuse ourselves so readily, it is difficult to discern the areas of oppression in our lives. After all, these are **our** thoughts, **our** attitudes, **our** perceptions – we justify and defend our thoughts with the same degree of intensity with which we justify and defend ourselves. As it is written,

> *'As a man thinketh in his heart, so is he.'*
>
> (Proverbs 23:7)

In other words, the essence of who we are is in our thought-life. Therefore, before any deliverance can truly be accomplished, we must honestly recognize and confess our need. We must stop pretending everything is 'all right'. We must humble ourselves and seek help. Indeed, as previously mentioned, the first stronghold that God must remove is pride. For until one is willing to admit that he needs deliverance, he will never be free from strongholds.

In order to recognize what is wrong in us, we must perceive God's standard of right. David in the height of ecstacy and Job in the pit of misery, as well as all of us in-between, have asked the same age-old question, *'What is man?'* The writer of Hebrews asks the same question, but then answers it under the inspiration of the Spirit. *'... We do see Him ... namely Jesus'* (Hebrews 2:9). Jesus Christ is the model of what God considers typical for the new-creation man (Ephesians 4:23–24). He is not just our Saviour, He is the Indwelling One who conforms us to His image, the first-born of a family of glorious sons (Hebrews 2:10; Romans 8:28–29).

But let us also realize that only Jesus can be like Jesus. As we yield to Him in increasing degrees of surrender, as we abide in Him and His Word abides in us, He brings forth life that is not simply 'like' His own; but is His very own life! Christ Himself living within us fulfils God's eternal purpose, which is to make man in His image. It is this coming forth in us of the Presence of the Lord Jesus that makes the weapons of our warfare mighty, empowering our words with authority as we pull down strongholds.

Therefore, you must learn to look objectively at any thoughts or attitudes that fail to conform to the likeness and teachings of Jesus. Those thoughts must be captured and wrong attitudes crucified. We must make way **in us** for the coming of the Lord. We must allow the 'increase of His government' to expand until we are so absorbed into His Spirit that we not only believe **in** Him, we believe **like** Him. His love, thoughts and desires flow out from within us.

Consequently, when we seek to identify and destroy demonic strongholds, the second fortress that must be annihilated is the stronghold of unbelief. It is this scheme of thinking that tells us Christlikeness is impossible, which holds all further spiritual growth hostage. This lie and the chains it places upon our hearts must be stripped from our lives.

Accordingly, take this moment and begin to pray in your spirit. Let the Holy Spirit rise and flood your heart. If you suffer from the stronghold which says you will never be like Christ, that stronghold can begin to come down right now. Let us pray:

'Lord Jesus, I submit to You. I declare, according to the Word of God, that because of Your power to subject all things unto Yourself, the weapons of my warfare are mighty to the pulling down of strongholds (2 Corinthians 10:3–4). I repent for using the lie, "I will never be like Jesus," as an excuse to sin and compromise my convictions. In Jesus' name, I renounce my flawed, sinful old nature and, by the grace of God and the power of Your Spirit, I pull down the stronghold of unbelief that exists in my mind. Because of the perfect sacrifice of Jesus Christ, I am a new creation. And I believe that I will go from glory to glory, being continually transformed into Christ's image as I walk with God.'

Defeat the Stronghold of Failure!

Let us look at other strongholds that may be in your life and see their origin and, more importantly, how they can be removed. First, remember that a stronghold is a house made of thoughts. Therefore, in regard to this type of warfare, Paul explained that our success is based upon taking '...*every thought captive to the obedience of Christ*...' (2 Corinthians 10:5). Since our goal is to allow the Spirit of Christ full access into our souls, we must capture our thoughts and make them Christ's slaves.

To deal with the stronghold of failure, we must make repentance our way of life. Bear in mind also that repentance means 'change', not merely remorse. Our thinking must change. There are herds of erroneous thoughts roaming across our minds, grazing upon the ever-available hay and stubble of unbelief and failure. Thoughts like, 'I will always be a failure', 'I am just a sinner', or 'I tried walking in the Spirit but it didn't work', converge and form the walls, floor and ceiling – the 'building material' of the stronghold of failure. To secure victory, you must capture these wrong thoughts.

Capture the thought: **'I am a failure!'** Repent of it, asking God to forgive you of your unbelief. Let your mind be renewed by the Word of God which states, *'I can do all things through Christ Who strengthens me.'* Even though you have failed and will probably fail again in the future, now because God is in your life you can confidently proclaim, 'Though I was a failure, my sufficiency comes from God, not myself. I am fully able to do all things through Christ Who strengthens me.'

Arrest the thought: **'I am just a sinner!'** Replace it with the confession of your faith which says, 'Though I was a sinner, now I am a beloved child of God and, though I occasionally still sin, the blood of Christ cleanses me of all unrighteousness' (1 John 1:9). Because of the blood, Christ's sacrifice makes each of us as pure as He is Himself. You are tearing down a stronghold of defeat that once oppressed you and you are beginning to replace it with the godly stronghold of faith, which is built upon the Word of God. With the old stronghold exposed and the thought-patterns of defeatism coming down, you are destroying the stronghold of failure in your life. As you continue being renewed in the spirit of your mind, by the Word of God, you will begin walking in tremendous power and peace. You will enter the godly stronghold of faith.

Let it be established in your attitudes that the goal and purpose of your salvation is that you be conformed to the likeness of Christ. Is it not written,

> *'Whom He foreknew, He also predestined to become conformed to the image of His Son, that He might be the first-born among many brethren?'* (Romans 8:29)

The same Lord who conquered the devil and liberated your

heart in salvation, is working still to renew your mind. While it is true that He is our promised land, it is also true that we are **His** promised land! **The giants within our hearts, though they have withstood and humbled us, shall not withstand Him! He is the eternal Joshua, the Holy One who knows no defeat!**

As long as we recognize that our salvation is a continual transformation, and that we are changing from *'glory to glory'* into the image of Christ, we should not be discouraged by the strongholds we discover; nor will occasional or momentary setbacks render us impotent. As we see our need, we rejoice in knowing it is only a matter of time before another giant is removed!

Destroying the Stronghold of Fear!

Another stronghold that oppresses men is fear. Your experience tells you that if you try something new, especially in front of people, you may be embarrassed and rejected. To counter this, a whole series of reactions emerges in your mind. You sit back when you should step forward. You are silent when you should be speaking! That silent, fearful withdrawal into yourself has become a house made of thoughts, wherein dwells a spirit of fear.

God does not want you in bondage. Therefore, let us look at some of the thoughts and experiences that may have formed the structure of this demonic fortress. Perhaps as a young child, when you attempted something new, the reaction among your family or friends was ridicule. Their thoughtless words went so deep that, in recoiling from the pain, you have involuntarily remained in the 'recoiled' or 'withdrawn' position. Since then, you have refused to place yourself in situations where you can become vulnerable to criticism. You may not even remember the incidents, but you have not stopped recoiling even until today.

Remember, Jesus said the Father would forgive us as we forgave others. As unjust as it may seem, your **reaction** to what hurt you was as far from the will of God as the actions were of those who hurt you. In fact, your reaction has actually become a part of your nature. You can be delivered from that oppression on your soul by releasing and forgiving those who hurt you. To the degree that you truly let the incident go and forgive the offender, to that same degree God will restore your soul to a balanced and healthy attitude toward people. As you increase in this process of forgiveness, you will grow in love and, as the Scripture says,

> *'There is no fear in love ... love casts out fear.'*
> (1 John 4:18)

The stronghold of fear will be replaced by the stronghold of love.

Always remember that **'Victory begins with the name of Jesus on our lips; but it will not be consummated until the nature of Jesus is in our hearts.'** It is not enough to have your *'house ... swept and put in order'* (Matthew 12:43); your thought-life must be **occupied** by the Person of Christ. But as you persist in yielding yourself to Christ, He will remove Satan's armour from your mind. He will show you what you need to bring down. You will see that the weapons of your warfare **are** mighty, to the pulling down of strongholds!

Chapter 5

Three Sources of Strongholds

If you want to identify the hidden strongholds in your life, you need only survey the attitudes in your heart. Every area in your thinking that glistens with hope in God is an area which is being liberated by Christ. But any system of thinking that does not have hope, which feels hopeless, is a stronghold which must be pulled down.

The First Source of Strongholds: The World

Generally speaking, strongholds originate from any one of three sources. The first is the very world into which we have been born. The steady stream of information and experience that continually shaped our childhood perceptions is the greatest source of strongholds within us. The amount of love (or lack of love) in our home, our cultural environment, peer values and pressures, as well as fears of rejection and exposure – even our physical appearance and intelligence, all combine to form our sense of identity and our view of life.

Our souls, wrought with insecurities, are highly sensitive to the criticisms and compliments of others. In the search to find oneself, such words are poured into young hearts like molten steel which, as they cool, are fused into our natures. How many of today's adults believe they are mentally slow simply because, as children, they absorbed into their self-concept the negative, thoughtless scolding of a teacher or parent?

These concepts and limitations are structured into us from childhood, built into our thinking patterns through the words and ideas of others. **Indeed, many of our opinions about life are ours only because we know of no other way to think.** Yet, we defend and protect our ideas, justifying our opinions as though they were born in the womb of our own creativity!

Another example of this is astrology. Multitudes of believers are subconsciously bound to the characteristics and weaknesses of their 'zodiac sign'. In their search for identity, this mixture of deceptive facts and illusions was absorbed into their soul, where it continues to stand even today in direct opposition to God's work of transformation.

As Christians, the only truth suitable for eternity is the truth of Christ. If we fail to realize this, we will only *'be like* [our] *teachers,'* never doing more than *'the deeds of* [our] *fathers'* (Luke 6:40; John 8:41). Our 'teachers' and 'fathers', more than likely, did the best they could. But our goal is not simply to do the deeds of our fathers, but to do the deeds of Jesus.

Therefore, Scripture instructs us to *'consider the outcome,'* or the end, of a man's way of life before we submit to his concepts of life (Hebrews 13:7). In so considering, it is obvious that only one Person, the Lord Jesus Christ, proved by His resurrection that He knew the secrets of life. By conquering death, He revealed He understood life.

Although Jesus will use people to teach us, we must not become followers of mere men where those men are not, indeed, conformed to Christ. Our goal must be conformity to Jesus Christ and Him only. Any teaching that does not support this singular purpose must not be allowed to rule us!

In this pilgrimage of the soul to find itself, we must surrender what we were to God, for unless we lose our lives to Jesus, we cannot find them. You see, when we come to Christ, all that we are in nature and character is destined to change. The Bible tells us God has provided for us a new heart, a new mind, a new spirit, a new nature and, ultimately, even a new name! (Hebrews 8:10; 1 Corinthians 2:16; 2 Corinthians 5:16–17; Revelation 2:17). Remember, when you were born again you received the very Spirit of God, and through His Spirit you were birthed into another realm: the Kingdom of Heaven. Though your feet are still on earth, through the vehicle of the Holy Spirit, you are united to the actual Person of Jesus Christ, Who is seated at the throne of God. Even as your limbs are attached to your torso, so your heart is attached to the power of God! You are never alone! Christ is always with you! What you were as a person prior to salvation, you will never be again!

The promise of God is

> *'If any man is in Christ, he is a new creature; the old things passed away; behold new things have come.'*
>
> (2 Corinthians 5:17)

Everything, even your intelligence and physical appearance, is now subject to change for the better. Old failures, prejudices and attitudes are destined to go; new faith and hope should be growing within you daily. How do we attain such a wonderful new beginning? We receive the Spirit of Christ into our hearts to empower us and we study the words of Christ to direct us; and whatever we find in us that is not like Jesus, we crucify it.

The Stronghold of Our Experiences

Another manner through which strongholds are built into us is through our experiences and the conclusions we have drawn from them. These experiences, for better or worse, are what we call reality. Let us realize that life, as we perceive it, is based upon whatever network of thoughts and opinions we are currently allowing to govern our souls. On the other hand, God defines reality as the 'Truth' found in His Word. For us to travel from our world into the reality of God, we must view Jesus' words as doors through which we enter God's eternal Kingdom. **In the combined meaning of all Jesus taught, we find the reality of the Kingdom of God.** Victory comes when we line ourselves up to the reality of God's life.

To topple the 'stronghold of our experiences' we must

> *'let God be found true, though every man be found a liar.'* (Romans 3:4)

The only One who has a right to shape our lives is Jesus Christ. We must determine to allow nothing and no one to shape us, not even our personal experiences, unless they are consistent with the promises of God.

In truth, who is ruling our lives, God or our experiences? To the degree that our experiences do not conform to the Word of God, they subtly teach us that God is not Who He says He is. We must guard our hearts and the opinions we form about life, for unless the events of our lives are consummated in Christlikeness, they are incomplete.

In other words, even though you were not healed, you should not conclude 'healing is not for today'. God's provision is **eternal**, which means that until heaven and earth pass away, He has provided for our healing. In regard to sin, though you repeatedly stumble, you must continue to believe God for grace to overcome. You must give yourself room to grow into new insights. You must never surrender your faith in God's Word! Experiences may seem valid, but if they have left you thinking that Jesus is not the same today as He was in the Gospels, the conclusion you have drawn is wrong. It is a stronghold that must be pulled down.

The Stronghold of Wrong Doctrines

A third source of strongholds comes from false church doctrines and teachings. Jesus warned,

'See to it no one misleads you.'   (Matthew 24:4)

We can be led by another person, but we must take responsibility that we are not **mis**led by that individual. We must study and know the Bible ourselves. If we do not, how can we discern error in the teaching we hear? As much as we love a particular pastor, as often as we have been edified by him, we must humbly ask the Lord to confirm any questionable doctrines. No teacher is so true, no prophet so pure that we can blindly let them lead us. They may lead us, but our eyes must be open and our ears sensitive to the confirming voice of Jesus. As it is written,

> *'Let every word be confirmed by the mouth of two or three witnesses.'*   (2 Corinthians 13:1)

Even true teachers can innocently communicate false doctrines. It does not matter how sincere our Bible teacher is. If what we are being taught does not lead us into Christ's love, His holiness, or His power; if we are not being prepared in these spiritual dimensions for Jesus and, through Him, for others, that doctrine is a stronghold which is limiting and oppressing us.

The safest way to insure that no one misleads us is to see to it we do not mislead ourselves. We must stay honest with God and sensitive to His love and His Word. Satan's plan is to make us somehow accept, either through our upbringing, our experiences or through church dogma, that certain portions of the life of Christ are untrue or not valid in our case. **Every battle we face in life is over the Word and whether or not we can build our lives upon the faithfulness and integrity of God.** If we hold fast to those things of which we are sure, God will be faithful to deliver us from every stronghold and lead us fully into His Kingdom.

Chapter 6

The Stronghold of Christ's Likeness

Victory begins with the name of Jesus on our lips. It is consummated by the nature of Jesus in our heart.

God's Highest Purpose

Most Christians only engage in spiritual warfare with a hope of either relieving present distresses or attaining a 'normal' existence. However, the purpose of all aspects of spirituality, warfare included, is to bring us into the image of Christ. Nothing, not worship nor warfare, neither love nor deliverance, is truly attainable if we miss the singular objective of our faith: Christlikeness.

Let us recall that the Lord delivered the ancient Hebrews **out** of Egypt so He could bring them **into** the Promised Land. Likewise, we are delivered **out** of sin, not that we might live for ourselves, but that we might **come** into Christlikeness. Our goals must align with God's, for if our nature does not change, we will invariably find ourselves entangled in the same problems that **caused** our difficulties in the first place.

While we may not want to hear this, many of our spiritual conflicts simply are not going to cease until the character of the Lord Jesus is formed in our hearts. The Father's goal in deliverance is much more than simply seeing our burdens or the devil taken off our backs. Indeed, the specific purpose toward which God steers the working of all things in our lives, is our conformity '...*to the image of His Son.*' The Father's purpose in our salvation was that Jesus would become '...*the first-born among many brethren*' (Romans 8:28–29). In other words, the way to realize God's ultimate victory is to reach toward His ultimate goal, which is complete transformation into the likeness of Christ.

There is a penetration of spirit between God and ourselves, where our spirits are fully saturated with the Living Presence of the Lord Jesus, where His glory so floods our lives that there is '...*no dark part*' left within us (Luke 11:36). This immediacy of the Lord's Presence produces an indestructible defense, a fortress within which we are hidden from evil. Through Him, we enter the excellence of His ways in our relationships, both with the Father and one another; thereby walking in immunity from countless satanic attacks. Indeed, as His fullness within us increases, then that which is written is fulfilled:

> '*As He is, so also are we in this world.*' (1 John 4:17)

and,

> '...*He Who is born of God keeps* [us] *and the evil one does not touch* [us].' (1 John 5:18 KJ)

We must realize that it is not Satan who defeats us; it is our **openness** to him. To perfectly subdue the devil we must walk in the '*shelter of the Most High*' (Psalm 91:1). Satan is tolerated for one purpose: the warfare between the devil and God's saints thrusts us into Christlikeness, where the nature of Christ becomes our only place of rest and security. God allows warfare to facilitate His eternal plan, which is to make man in His image (Genesis 1:26).

Once we realize that the Father's goal is to transform our lives with Christ's life, we will continually find that God has one answer to spiritual warfare: **appropriate the nature of His Son!** Are you troubled by demons of fear or doubt? Submit **those** areas to God, repenting of your unbelief and then yielding yourself to Christ's faith within you. Are you troubled with spirits of lust and shame? Present those very areas of sin to God, repenting of your old nature, drawing upon the forgiveness of Christ and His purity of heart.

The Father is more concerned with the coming forth of His Son in our lives than He is in defeating Satan. Who is the devil, that he can defy the Living God? Indeed, it is of the greatest truth that, once the devil recognizes his assault against your life has not pulled you from God, but **toward** Him, once he perceives that his temptations are actually forcing you to appropriate the virtue of Christ, the enemy will withdraw.

The Goal is Christlikeness, Not Warfare

There is a time, which we will speak of later in this book, when the Lord will call us to pull down the strongholds of hell over our churches and our communities. There is another time, however, when to engage in much spiritual warfare is actually a **distraction** from your obedience to God. Jesus defeated Satan in Gethsemane and the cross, not by directly confronting the devil, but by fulfilling the destiny to which He had been called at Calvary. **The greatest battle that was ever won was accomplished by the apparent death of the victor, without even a word of rebuke to His adversary!** The prince of this world was judged and principalities and powers were disarmed not by confrontational warfare, but by the surrender of Jesus Christ on the cross.

There are occasions when your battle against the devil is actually a digression from the higher purpose God has for you. Intercessors and warfare captains take note: there is a demon whose purpose is to lure one's mind into hell. It's name is 'Wrong Focus'. If you are continually seeing evil spirits in people or in the material world around you, you may actually be fighting this spirit. The ultimate goal of this demon is to produce mental illness in saints who move in deliverance. **Listen very carefully: we are not called to focus on the battle or the devil, except where that battle hinders our immediate transformation into Christ's likeness.** Our calling is to focus on Jesus. The work of the devil, however, is to draw our eyes from Jesus. Satan's first weapon always involves luring our eyes from Christ. Turn to Jesus and almost immediately the battle vanishes.

I knew a man once who owned a record company. Besides running the operation, he also spent many hours in production listening to the 'mother disk', which was the record from which all subsequent records were pressed. Over the years, his ears became adept at catching the 'pops and sizzles', the imperfections that had to be eliminated in the master disk. I remarked one day that I thought working with music must be enjoyable. His response was enlightening. He said, 'You know, I haven't listened to music in years. When I turn on my sophisticated home stereo, no matter what recording I'm listening to, all I hear are the "pops and sizzles".'

In the same way his thoughts were bent toward musical imperfections, so Wrong Focus will seek to turn your thoughts continually toward the enemy. Suddenly, all you will see are demons. The true gift called 'discerning of spirits' is a balanced gift which enables you to recognize at least as many angelic spirits as you do evil spirits. The proper manifestation of this gift has a much more positive focus and influence than what commonly masquerades as discernment.

An example of the proper balance in discernment is seen in Second Kings. The Syrian army had surrounded a city in Israel, much to the consternation of the servant of the prophet Elisha. To calm his fright, Elisha prayed that his servant's eyes would be opened. He then encouraged his servant, saying,

*'Do not fear, for **those who are with us** are more than **those who are with them**.'* (2 Kings 6:16)

As the Lord opened the servant's eyes, he saw what Elisha saw:

> *'The mountain was full of horses and chariots of fire all around Elisha.'* (2 Kings 6:17)

In spiritual warfare, the battle is never limited to an 'us against them' human affair. It always includes *'those ... with us'* against *'those ... with them'*. True discernment is as fully aware of the vast multitude of angels loyal to God, as it is aware of the activity of the demonic realm – and it is aware that the angelic hosts on our side are both stronger and more numerous than the enemy. Remember, if you fail to 'hear the music' in your times of warfare, your discernment is, at best, incomplete.

We must learn that, on a personal level, it is better to develop godly virtues than to spend our day praying against the devil. Indeed, it is the **joy of the Lord** that casts out spirits of depression. It is our **living faith** which destroys spirits of unbelief; it is **aggressive love** which casts out fear.

As we continually yield ourselves to Christ, surrendering ourselves by faith to His nature and His words, we literally build the impenetrable stronghold of His Presence around us. The way into the fortress of the Almighty is simple. **Victory begins with the name of Jesus on our lips. It is consummated by the nature of Jesus in our heart.**

Chapter 7

Rule in the Midst of Your Enemies!

Our peace does not come from extreme indifference, nor is it from becoming so 'spiritual' that you fail to notice a problem. It is being so confident in God's love that you know, regardless of the battle and the difficulties in your circumstances, that *'greater is He who is in you than he who is in the world'* (1 John 4:4). You are not self-assured, you are God-assured.

The God of Peace Will Crush Satan

To wage effective spiritual warfare, we must understand spiritual authority. Spiritual authority is not forcing your will upon another. When you have spiritual authority, you have established God's peace in an area that once was full of conflict and oppression. Therefore, to truly be able to move in authority, we must first have peace.

The Apostle Paul taught,

> *'...the God of Peace will soon crush Satan under your feet.'* (Romans 16:20)

When we maintain peace during warfare it is a crushing death blow to satanic oppression and fear. Our victory never comes from our emotions or our intellect. Our victory comes by refusing to judge by what our eyes see or our ears hear, and by trusting that what God has promised will come to pass.

We will never know Christ's victory in its fullness until we stop reacting humanly to our circumstances. **When you truly have authority over something you can look at that thing without worry, fear or anxiety.** Your peace is the proof of your victory. Jesus' authority over the violent storm (Matthew 8:23–27) was the exercise and expansion of His peace over the elements. He did not fight against the storm, nor did He fear it. He faced its fury and subdued it with His authority, in perfect peace. In Pilate's court, in a world stirred to an emotional frenzy by the powers of hell, a holy tranquillity surrounded Christ – a peace that was born out of His resolve to do God's will no matter what the cost. His Spirit emanated a calm that perfectly represented the peace at God's throne. In a matter of moments it was no longer Jesus who was on trial, but Satan, Pilate and the nation of Israel.

Satan's arsenal consists of such things as fear, worry, doubt, self-pity, etc. Every one of these weapons robs us of peace and leaves us troubled inside. Do you want to discern where the enemy is coming against you? In the network of your relationships, wherever you do not have peace, you have war. Conversely, wherever you have victory, you have peace. When Satan hurls his darts against you, **the more peace you have during adversity, the more truly you are walking in Christ's victory**.

Paul tells us to be

> '... *in no way alarmed by your opponents – which is a sign of destruction for them, but of salvation for you.*'
>
> (Philippians 1:28)

Your peace, your immovable stand upon the Word of God is a sign that you are positioned correctly in perfect submission to the will of God. The very fact that you are '*in no way alarmed*' by your adversary is a sign that you have authority over him.

Peacemakers are Sons of God

Peace is Spirit Power. A peacemaker is not merely someone who protests against war; he is one who is inwardly so yielded to Christ in spirit and purpose that He can be called a 'son of God'. Where he goes, God goes and where God goes, he goes. He is fearless, calm and bold. Peace emanates from him the way light and heat radiate from fire.

In the battles of life, your peace is actually a weapon. Indeed, your confidence declares that you are not falling for the lies of the devil. You see, the first step toward having spiritual authority over the adversary is having peace in spite of our circumstances. When Jesus confronted the devil, He did not confront Satan with His emotions or in fear. Knowing that the devil was a liar, He simply refused to be influenced by any other voice than God's. His peace overwhelmed Satan, His authority then shattered the lie, which sent demons fleeing.

Rest Before Rule

In the 23rd Psalm David declares,

> *'Yea, though I walk through the valley of the shadow of death, I fear no evil; for Thou art with me...'*

There is a place of walking with God where you simply fear no evil. David faced a lion, a bear and a giant. In this psalm he stood in the *'shadow of death'* itself, yet he *'feared no evil.'* David's trust was in the Lord. He said, *'...for Thou art with me.'* Because God is with you, every adversity you face will unfold in victory as you maintain your faith in God! David continued,

> *'...Thou dost prepare a table before me in the presence of my enemies.'*

The battle you are in will soon become a meal to you, an experience that will nourish and build you up spiritually.

Only God's peace will quell your fleshly reactions in battle. The source of God's peace is God Himself. Indeed,

> *'Before the throne there was, as it were, a sea of glass like crystal...'* (Revelation 4:6a)

The glass sea is a symbol: there are no ripples, no waves, no anxieties troubling God. The Lord is never worried, never in a hurry nor without an answer. The sea around Him is perfectly still and totally calm. All our victories flow out from being seated here with Him.

God is our Father. The Heavenly Jerusalem is our mother, the birthplace of our new nature (Galatians 4:26). And you, you are a beloved child of God, part of the Father's family and a member of His household (Ephesians 2:19). You must know by revelation that you are not struggling to get up into Heaven; rather, you were born there in spiritual rebirth (John 3:1–8 Amplified). You must be settled and positioned correctly in your relationship with the Almighty.

To those who have been born again from above, He says,

> *'...Sit at My right hand while I make thy enemies a footstool for thy feet.'* (Psalm 110:1–2)

Before you go into warfare, recognize that it is not you that the devil is afraid of, it is **Christ in you!** We have been raised up and seated with Christ in heavenly places (Ephesians 2:6). This is why the Holy Spirit continues to speak to us that worship of God is our first response in battle. Position yourself in the Presence of God. Sit, at rest, in the knowledge that Christ **has already** made your enemies the footstool for your feet. From the position of rest, the Word of the Lord continues,

> *'The Lord will stretch forth Thy strong scepter from Zion saying, "Rule in the midst of Thine enemies."'* (Psalm 110:2)

Rest precedes rule. Peace precedes power. Do not seek to rule over the devil until you are submitting to God's rule over you. The focal point of all victory comes from seeking God until you find Him, and having found Him, allowing His Presence to fill your spirit with His peace. From full assurance at His right hand, as we rest in His victory, let us rule in the midst of our enemies.

PART TWO:

The Battleground of the Church

The other churches in our cities are not our enemies! We must learn to war against the illusions and strife, the fears and jealousies that are sent from hell to divide us. If Jesus is eternally praying for our oneness (John 17:20–23), then we must recognize that Satan is continually fighting against it. The devil knows that when we become one with Christ and, through Him, one with each other, it is only a matter of time before this Jesus-built church will destroy the empire of hell!

Chapter 8

The Lord Whose Sword is Drawn

Of all the names that the Heavenly Father could have given His Son, it is most significant that He chose the name 'Jesus', for Jesus is the Greek form of 'Joshua', who was the Hebrew general who led the people into warfare. To be prepared for greater victories, we need a greater revelation of Jesus Christ; we need to see Him as He will be revealed in the last moments of this age: a Holy Warrior, dressed for battle.

Will You Recognize Jesus When He Comes?

'Now it came about when Joshua was by Jericho, that he lifted up his eyes and looked, and behold, a man was standing opposite him with his sword drawn in his hand, and Joshua went to him and said to him, "Are you for us or for our adversaries?"' (Joshua 5:13)

There is something about the time just prior to a move of God that causes many to wonder if the Lord is for them or against them. He seems confrontational, too intense, too 'different' from the One we had learned to trust. Yet, during these last few years, this is exactly the situation in the Lord's relationship with the church. The Lord has stood before us with His sword drawn. Perhaps you have been through a time where the tip of Christ's sword seemed aimed straight at your heart.

Let me reassure you, God is for you. In fact, it is His expressed purpose to release this same sword of the Spirit, which is the Word of God (Ephesians 6:17), through your words and prayers. But before the Lord's sword will come through your mouth, it must first pass through your heart. God must confront the stronghold of fear within us before we can be effective against the enemy in the heavenly places.

Do not withdraw or be terrified at this new unveiling of the Son of God, for it is, in fact, the beginning of God fitting you for battle. By the time you are fully trained, you will be a fearless warrior in His army. Currently, however, we are a pampered, undisciplined people who have not understood the day of warfare that looms before us. We must realize that in the last moments of this age, to prepare us for the raging of Satan as his time shortens (Revelation 12:12), the Lord Jesus will raise an army to whom He will be revealed in a manner unfamiliar to most Christians.

Isaiah tells us that,

> *'The Lord will go forth like a warrior, He will arouse His zeal like a man of war. He will utter a shout, yes, He will raise a war cry. He will prevail against His enemies.'*　　　　　　　　　　(Isaiah 42:13)

We have known the Lord as our Saviour and our Shepherd. These revelations of our beloved Lord are no less true because a new aspect of His nature is revealed. It is simply that this new dimension is so startlingly different from how we have known Him. Be of good cheer, this frightening Warrior King, with His sword drawn, with the shout of war upon His lips, is the same Blessed Saviour Who died on the cross for our sins.

Yet, in truth, we cannot soften the shock of this next unveiling of Christ. Your immediate dismay shall be in no way less dramatic than that which was revealed to Joshua on the plains of Jericho. Your concepts will be shaken and fears confronted.

Looking again at Joshua, truly he had already known the Lord in a wonderful, intimate way in the wilderness tabernacle. But here, standing before him, was a new revelation of Christ. The Lord Himself had come to lead His people into war. Ultimately, these refugees from Egypt and their wilderness children would defeat many nations stronger and more numerous than themselves (Deuteronomy 9:1). They would do the impossible through the power of the Lord.

Joshua was alarmed, but both Joshua and the people with him were more prepared for this battle than even they realized. Their time in the wilderness had conditioned them for war. Likewise, the wilderness you have been in has not been a punishment, but a time of preparation and of learning obedience. You have watched in fear the spiritual death of church leaders who disobeyed the Lord. But you have not stumbled over their disobedience; **you have learned from it!**

Before Jesus returns, those who have passed the wilderness tests will receive another revelation: Christ will be revealed to them as *'Captain of the host.'* They will be ready to follow the Lamb wherever He goes.

> *'And Joshua fell on his face to the earth, and bowed down, and said to Him, "What has my lord to say to His servant?" And the captain of the Lord's host said to Joshua, "Remove your sandals from your feet, for the place where you are standing is holy." And Joshua did so.'* (Joshua 5:14–15)

This new unveiling of the Lord is holy. Do not gainsay or criticize what you may not fully understand! We are beginning to perceive the Lord as He truly is and as He will be revealed in the days ahead.

The promise of the Lord, which we read earlier, is that He *'...will go forth like a warrior ... He will raise a war cry. He will prevail against His enemies.'* Within the ranks of the Advancing Church, Jesus is raising a war cry. Can you hear His shout in the intercession? There is new authority being raised up, a new generation whose voice thunders with the cry of prophetic prayer. Through the church, Christ Himself is prevailing against His enemies! Indeed, the gates of hell shall not stand against the church Jesus is building! (Matthew 16:18) The hour has come for His church to grow in all aspects into Him, who is our head, even Christ, **the Warrior King!** (Ephesians 4:15).

Chapter 9

Beware of the Stronghold of Cold Love

Is your love growing and becoming softer, brighter, more daring and more visible? Or is it becoming more discriminating, more calculating, less vulnerable and less available? This is a very important issue, for your Christianity is only as real as your love is. A measurable decrease in your ability to love is evidence that a stronghold of cold love is developing within you.

Guard Against Unforgiveness!

'Because lawlessness is increased, most people's love will grow cold.' (Matthew 24:12)

A major area of spiritual warfare that has come against the church is the sphere of church relationships. Satan knows that a church divided against itself cannot stand. We may enjoy temporary blessings and seasonal break-throughs, but to win a city-wide war, Jesus is raising up a united, city-wide church. An earmark of this corporate, overcoming church will be its commitment to love. Yet, because of the increasing iniquity in the end of this age, true Christian love will be severely assaulted.

There is no spiritual unity, and hence no lasting victory,

without love. Love is a passion for oneness. Bitterness, on the other hand, is characterized by a noticeable lack of love. This cold love is a demonic stronghold. In our generation cold love is becoming increasingly more common. It shuts down the power of prayer and disables the flow of healing and outreach. In fact, where there is persistent and hardened unforgiveness in a person or church, the demonic world (known in Matthew 18:34 as 'torturers') has unhindered access.

The Scriptures warn that even a little root of bitterness in a person's life can spring up and defile many (Hebrews 12:15). **Bitterness is unfulfilled revenge.** Another's thoughtlessness or cruelty may have wounded us deeply. It is inevitable that, in a world of increasing harshness and cruelty, you will at some time be hurt. But if you fail to react with love and forgiveness, if you retain in your spirit the debt the offender owes you, that offense will rob your heart of its capacity to love. Imperceptibly, you will become a member of the majority of end-time Christians whose love is '*growing cold*'.

Bitterness is a classic symptom of the stronghold of cold love. To deal with this, you must repent of this attitude and forgive the one who hurt you. This painful experience was allowed by God to teach you how to love your enemies. If you still have unforgiveness toward someone who hurt you, you have failed this test. Fortunately, this was just a test, not a final exam. You actually need to thank God for the opportunity to grow in divine love. Thank Him that your whole life is not being swallowed up in bitterness and resentment. Millions of souls are swept off into eternal judgment every day without any hope of escaping from embitterment, but you have been given God's answer for your pain. God gives you a way out: **love!**

As you embrace God's love and begin to walk in forgiveness, you are actually pulling down the stronghold of bitterness and its manifestation of cold love in your life. Because of this experience, you will eventually have more love than you ever did. You truly do need to thank God.

Love Without Commitment is Not Love

> *'And at that time many will fall away and will betray one another and hate one another. And many false prophets will arise, and will mislead many. And because lawlessness is increased, the love of many will grow cold.'* (Matthew 24:10–12)

I want to make it perfectly clear: there is no such thing as love without commitment. The measure of your love is found in the depth of your commitment. How often I have heard people tell me, 'I loved once, but I was hurt.' Or, 'I was committed to Christian service, but they used me.' People withdraw from being committed, never realizing that their love is growing cold! It may not **seem** like they have become cold – they still go to church, read the Bible, tithe, sing and look like Christians – but inside they have become distant and aloof from other people. They have withdrawn from the love of God.

Jesus said, *'Stumbling blocks are inevitable...'* (Matthew 18:7). In your walk there will be times when even good people have bad days. As long as you live on earth, there will never be a time when 'stumbling blocks' cease to be found upon your path. **People do not stumble over boulders, but over stones, little things.** To stumble is to stop walking and fall. Have you stumbled over someone's weakness or sin lately? Have you gotten back up and continued loving as you did before, or has that fall caused you to withdraw somewhat from walking after love? To preserve the quality of love in your heart, you must forgive those who have caused you to stumble.

Every time you refuse to forgive or fail to overlook a weakness in another, your heart not only hardens toward them, it hardens toward God. You cannot form a negative opinion of someone (even though they may deserve it!) and allow that opinion to crystalize into an attitude. For every time you do, an aspect of your heart will cool toward God. You may still think you are open to God, but the Scriptures are clear:

'... the one who does not love his brother whom he has seen, cannot love God whom he has not seen.'

(1 John 4:20)

You may not like what someone has done, but you do not have an option to stop loving them. Love is your only option.

What do I mean by love? First, I do not merely mean 'tough love'. I mean gentle, affectionate, sensitive, open, persistent love. God will be tough when He needs to be, and we will be firm when He tells us to be, but beneath our firmness must be an underground river of love waiting to spring into action. By 'love' I mean a compassion that is empowered by faith and prayer to see God's best come forth in the one I love. When I have love for someone, I have predetermined that I am going to stand with them, regardless of what they are going through.

We each need people who are committed to us as individuals; people who know we are not perfect, but love us anyway. The manifestation of God's Kingdom will not come without people being committed to each other to reach God's fullness. We are not talking about salvation; we are talking about growing up in that salvation until we love and are committed to each other with Jesus' love.

Many people will stumble over little faults and human weaknesses. These minor things are quickly pumped up by the enemy into great big problems. Oh, how frail are the excuses people use to justify withdrawing from others! In reality, these problems, often with a church or pastor, are a smokescreen which mask the person's lack of love.

We need to overcome our hang-ups about commitment, for no one will attain the fullness of God's purposes on earth without being committed to imperfect people along the way.

'Well, as soon as I find a church that believes as I do, I will be committed.' This is a dangerous excuse, because as soon as you decide you do not want to forgive, or God begins to deal with the quality of your love, you will blame your withdrawing on some minor doctrinal difference. The Kingdom of God is not based on mere doctrines, it is founded upon **relationships** – relationships with God and, because of God, with one another. Doctrines only help define those relationships. We are not 'anti-doctrine', but we are against **empty** doctrines, which seem like virtues but are simply excuses that justify cold love.

The Greatest Commandments

An expert in the Law once asked Jesus which was the greatest commandment. His reply was wonderful. He said,

> ' "You shall love the Lord your God with all your heart, and with all your soul, and with all your mind, and with all your strength." The second is like the first, "You shall love your neighbor as yourself." '
>
> (Mark 12:28–29)

Jesus then said that *'the second commandment is like the first.'* When you love God, your love for others will be like your love for God: the **'second is like the first'**. The more you unconditionally love God, the more you will unconditionally love others.

To those whose attitude is 'just Jesus and me' I say, it is wonderful you found Jesus. But you cannot truly have Jesus and simultaneously not do what He says. **The outgrowth of love and faith in Christ is love and faith like Christ's**, which means we are committed, even as He is, to His people.

You see, the Kingdom of God is not in you or in me. It is in **us**, corporately. We are being perfected into a unit (John 17). To have the Kingdom, we must be committed to one another as individuals and as churches. If Christ accepts us while we are still imperfect, we must also accept one another. **The people who possess the Kingdom of God in its reality are people who overcome the obstacles of each other's faults.** They help each other become what God has called them to be: the living body of Jesus Christ.

Remember, the goal of pulling down the stronghold of cold love is to see the oneness of Christ's body revealed. You will be challenged in this, but if you persist, you will discover the heights and depths, the length and breadth of Christ's love. You will become a body filled and flooded with God Himself.

Chapter 10

The Gift of Discernment

The Spirit will speak in dreams, visions and prophetic words, but much of what will be revealed will actually come through our capacity to perceive correctly. The Scriptures tell us that Jesus perceived the thoughts of men 'in His Spirit'. So also with us, if we will move in divine discernment, our view of life must be purged of human thoughts and reactions.

To Discern You Cannot Judge

The beginning of true discernment will not come until we crucify our instincts to judge. This takes many months, and usually years, of uprooting all thought-systems that have not been planted in the divine soil of faith and love for people. To appropriate the discernment which is in the *'mind of Christ'* (1 Corinthians 2:16), we must first find the heart of Christ. The heart and love of Jesus is summed up in His own words:

> *'...I did not come to judge the world, but to save the world.'*
> (John 12:47)

Spiritual discernment is the grace to see into the unseen. It is a gift **of the Spirit** to perceive what is **in the spirit**. Its purpose is to see into the nature of that which is veiled. But the first veil which must be removed is the veil over our own hearts. We must see ourselves and the measure of our need. For the capacity to see into that which is **outside** comes from Christ revealing that which is **inside**. Jesus demands we understand our own need of His mercy so that, out of the grace which we have received, we can compassionately minister to others. In this process, we will discover the depravity and selfishness of our carnal nature. We will know thoroughly that the gift of discernment is not a faculty of our minds.

We must ever be conscious that Christ's goal is to save, not judge. We are called to navigate the narrow and well-hidden path into the true nature of men's needs. If we would truly help men, we must remember, we are following a Lamb.

This foundation must be laid correctly, for if you will discern, you cannot react. To perceive, you must make yourself blind to what seems apparent. People may react to you, but you cannot react to them. You must always remain forgiving in nature, for the demons you would cast out will speak to you in the voice of the man, masquerading as the man himself. For this very reason Jesus said,

> *'Whoever shall speak a word against the Son of Man, it shall be forgiven him.'* (Mark 3:28)

Jesus was prepared in His heart to forgive men **before** they ever sinned against Him. **He knew His mission was to die for men, not condemn them.**

We are not only called into Christ's life, but into His mission as well. Jesus said,

> *'As Thou didst send Me into the world, I also have sent them...'* (John 17:18)

We are called to die that others may live. Therefore, we must realize that before our perception develops, our love must develop until our normal attitude is one of forgiveness. If God will show us the hearts of men, and use us to release them from captivity, we cannot react to what they say. As our perception becomes more like Christ Himself and men's hearts are revealed to us, we cannot even react to what they **think**.

If we do not move in divine forgiveness, we will walk in much deception. We will presume we have discernment when, in truth, we are seeing through the veil of a 'critical spirit'. We must know our weaknesses, for if we are blind to our sins, what we assume we discern in men will merely be the reflection of ourselves. Indeed, if we do not move in love, we will actually become a menace to the body of Christ.

This is exactly what Jesus taught when He said,

> '*Do not judge, lest you be judged. For in the way you judge, you will be judged; and by your standard of measure, it shall be measured to you. And why do you look at the speck in your brother's eye, but do not notice the log that is in your own? Or how can you say to your brother, "Let me take the speck out of your eye," and behold, the log is in your own eye?*
>
> '*You hypocrite, first take the log out of your own eye; and then you shall see clearly enough to take the speck out of your brother's eye.*'   (Matthew 7:1–3, 5)

Repentance is the removal of the 'logs' within our vision; **it is the true beginning of seeing clearly**. There are many who suppose they are receiving the Lord's discernment concerning one thing or another. Perhaps in some things they are; only God knows. But many are simply judging others and calling it discernment. Jesus **commanded** us to judge not. The same Eternal hand that wrote the Law on stones in the Old Covenant is writing the Law of the Kingdom on tablets of flesh today. This word to '*judge not*' is just as immutably final as His Ten Commandments. It is still **God** speaking.

The Goal is to See Clearly

The judgmental carnal mind always sees the image of itself in others. Without realizing it is seeing itself, it assumes it is perceiving others. Jesus refers to the person who judges as a *'hypocrite'*. The Lord is not saying we should totally stop thinking about people. He wants us to be able to help one another. The emphasis in Jesus' command to *'judge not'* is summarized in His concluding remark:

> *'First take the log out of your own eye and **then** you will see clearly to take the speck out of your brother's eye.'*

The way we help is not by judging, but by **seeing clearly!** And we do not see clearly until we have been through deep and thorough repentance; until the instinct to judge after the flesh is uprooted!

We have seen that Jesus paralleled speaking to people about their sins with taking specks out of their eyes. The eye is the most tender, most sensitive part of the human body. How do you take a speck out of someone's eye? Very carefully! You must win their trust. This means consistently demonstrating an attitude that does not judge, that will not instinctively condemn. To help people, we must see clearly. We must be able to see where a person's vision is obstructed, develop trust between us and remove their *'speck'* without judging or condemning them.

If you seek to have a heart that does not condemn; if you truly crucify your instinct to judge, you will have laid a true foundation for the gift of discernment, for you will have prepared your heart to receive the dreams, visions and insights from God. You will be unstained by human bias and corruption.

Chapter 11

Eliminating False Discernment

If what you have to say to someone is very important, you will not let them continue their labours while you talk. You ask for their undivided attention. So also God does not speak to us until we slow down, tune out the static and give Him our attention. To walk in true discernment, our hearts must be quiet before God. We must learn how to listen.

Cease Striving and Know

God wants us to learn how to wait and listen. We read of the Lord's command in the Psalms:

> *'Be still and know that I am God.'* (Psalm 46:10)

We cannot engage in spiritual warfare without first being conscious of God and, through Him, discerning the enemy. All true discernment comes through a heart that has ceased striving, a heart that knows, even in the fiery trial of its personal struggle, that the Lord is God.

There is a 'jamming station' that inhibits our powers of discernment. Our **thoughts** and **reactions** block us from hearing God. Until the motor of the carnal mind is turned off, true discernment will not consistently be ours. We must die to personal judgments, ideas of retaliation and self-motivation. Indeed, Jesus said,

> *'I can do nothing on My own initiative, as I hear, I judge.'* (John 5:30)

He *'ceased striving'*. We also must learn to **listen** to the voice of the Holy Spirit. As we stop our striving, **as we hear**, we judge and discern.

Abounding Love Brings Discernment With it

> *'I pray that your love may abound still more and more in real knowledge and all discernment...'*
> (Philippians 1:9)

Discernment comes from abounding love. What is abounding love? It is love that leaps out from us toward others. It is motivated by long-term commitment; it is anointed by sacrificial charity.

There is a false discernment that is based on mistrust, suspicion and fear. You can recognize false discernment by the coldness around it. False discernment may be packaged in a type of love, but it does not originate in love; it comes out of criticism. True discernment is rooted deeply in love.

Picture, if you will, a long-haired young man. His clothes are unkempt and he has tattoos on his arms. It is night and he is walking toward you on a lonely street. It is easy to judge such a person after the obvious and superficial. Now look at this young man in the same setting, but as his mother. You can still see his outer appearance, but when you look at him, you have **insight** into his life and **hope** for his future. You see a little boy growing up without a father, a child rejected often by his friends. You have a commitment toward this man that runs deep, that has been sustained by love, that you have carried since you suffered in giving him birth.

False discernment sees the **outside** of the person or situation and pretends it knows the **inside**. Their judgments are false because they are not committed to the washing of the church; neither are they willing to labour for her and give her birth! Godly discernment comes from having godly motives; godly motives are those rooted in committed love.

> *'Do not judge according to appearance, but judge with righteous judgment.'*　　　　　　　　　(John 7:24)

Righteous judgment is the direct result of love. If you cannot pray in love for a person or the church, do not presume you have true discernment. **Love precedes peace, and peace precedes perception.** Without love and peace in your heart, your judgment will be overly harsh. Regardless of the smile upon your face, your heart will have too much anger. False discernment is always slow to hear, quick to speak and quick to anger.

Peace Must Rule Our Hearts

There is a tension underlying false discernment, an anxiety that pressures the mind to make a judgment. True discernment emerges out of a tranquil and pure heart, one that is almost surprised by the wisdom and grace in the voice of God. Remember, our thoughts will always be coloured by the attitudes of our hearts. Jesus said,

> *'Out of the abundance of the heart the mouth speaketh.'*
> 　　　　　　　　　　　　　　　(Matthew 12:34 KJ)

He also said,

> *'Out of the heart of men proceed evil thoughts.'*
> 　　　　　　　　　　　　　　　(Mark 7:21)

Again He said,

> *'... the pure in heart ... shall see God.'*
> 　　　　　　　　　　　　　　　(Matthew 5:8)

From the heart the mouth speaks, the eyes see and the mind thinks. In fact, Proverbs 4:23 tells us that '... *out of the heart flow the issues of life.*'

Life, as we know it, is based upon the condition of our heart. This is very important because the gifts of the Spirit must pass through our hearts before they are presented to the world around us. In other words, if our hearts are not right, the gifts will not be right either.

When the heart has unrest it cannot hear from God. Therefore, we must learn to **mistrust** our judgment when our heart is bitter, angry, ambitious or harbouring strife for any reason. The Scripture tells us to allow

> '*the peace of Christ to rule* [act as arbiter] *in our hearts.*'
> (Colossians 3:15)

To hear clearly from God, we must first have peace.

Solomon wrote,

> '*One hand full of tranquillity is better than two fists full of labor and striving after the wind.*'
> (Ecclesiastes 4:6)

There is too much labour and toil in our minds, too much striving after the wind. If we want discernment we must become aggressively calm. This is not a passive state of mind, but an expectant, focused, waiting upon God. Discernment comes from our sensitivity to Christ in the realm of the Spirit. It comes from love in our motivation, peace in our hearts and a poised and waiting attitude of mind toward God. Through a life so prepared by God, the gift of discernment is revealed.

Chapter 12

Repairers of the Breach

'And those from among you will rebuild the ancient
ruins;
'You will raise up the age-old foundations;
'And you will be called the repairer of the breach,
'The restorer of the paths in which to dwell.'

(Isaiah 58:12)

The Gathering Together of the Saints

Most of true Christianity shares a doctrine commonly called
the 'rapture' of the church (1 Thessalonians 4:16). And
while study and debate surround the timing of this event,
Scripture assures us that it will occur before Jesus Himself
returns. However, before the rapture occurs, there will be a
time of unusual grace in which the living church of Jesus
Christ, like a bride, *'...makes herself ready'* (Revelation
19:7). In this unparalleled season of preparation, those who
are alive in Christ shall realize a level of holiness and
blamelessness of the quality in which Jesus Himself walked
(1 Thessalonians 3:11–13; Ephesians 5:26–27; Philippians
1:9–10).

The result of this new level of holiness will be a new level
of unity. Fault-finding and gossip will disappear. In their
place will be intercession and love. Wholeness will return to
the church. This also means that the ambition and division

we see today between congregations will be identified as sins, which will be repented of before Jesus returns.

The truth of this message must be made clear, for most Christians consider oneness within the body inconceivable before Jesus returns. They have not discerned nor warred against the spirit of Antichrist, which has conditioned believers to accept strife and sectarianism in the church. **The church which will ultimately be raptured will be a church free of strife and carnal divisions.**

During the rapture our bodies will be changed. But our **character**, that is, the essence of who we have become, will remain intact. There will be no regrets or wondering how 'those from that church' made it, for the living bride will be a church built together in love, meeting in separate buildings but serving the single Lord. The true disciples of the Lord Jesus will be known for their intense and holy love for one another – not merely in their individual local assemblies, but within the context of a city-wide church.

It is highly significant that the Scriptural term for the rapture is called *'the gathering together'* (2 Thessalonians 2:1; Matthew 24:31). What ultimately will be consummated in our gathering together **physically** to the Lord will be precipitated by a **spiritual** gathering together of His body on earth. Concerning the *'...end of the age,'* Jesus taught that the *'good fish'* shall be *'gathered ... into containers'* (Matthew 13:48). In the context of spiritual warfare, Jesus warned, *'...he who does not gather with Me, scatters'* (Matthew 12:30).

This scattering, dividing process among the Lord's sheep has gone on long enough. Jesus has set His heart to bring healing and unity to His body. In this regard, through the prophet Jeremiah, the Lord spoke a sombre warning. He said,

> *'Woe to the shepherds who are destroying and scattering the sheep of My pasture!'* (Jeremiah 23:1)

Jesus is not pleased with the carnal divisions in His body!

Indeed, there will be a time of punishment, and that soon coming, in which the Lord will chasten those pastors who continue to build their kingdoms, without labouring together to build His. To them He says,

> *'I am about to attend to you for the evil of your deeds.'*
> (Jeremiah 23:2)

In the tenth chapter of John, the Lord makes His goal clear: there shall be *'one flock with one Shepherd'* (John 10:16). He reveals it is the wolf nature which *'...snatches* [the sheep] *and scatters them'*; and it is the hireling nature which allows the scattering to occur. But His promise to His sheep says this:

> *'Then I Myself shall gather the remnant of My flock ... and they will be fruitful and multiply. I shall also raise up shepherds over them and they will tend them and they will not be afraid any longer ... nor will any be missing.'*
> (Jeremiah 23:3–4)

The pastors of the last Christian Church will be under-shepherds to the Lord Jesus; they will be anointed to gather together His remnant and under that anointing shall be *'fruitful and multiply.'*

Indeed, right now, in the context of humbling ourselves and submitting our hearts to His will, we are participating in being *'gathered together'*. And that process will progressively increase until the barriers between brethren are melted by the overcoming nature of Christ's love. Before Jesus returns, we will truly be *'one flock with one Shepherd.'* We will be a holy and blameless sheepfold, meeting in different buildings, but baptized into one body.

Do Not Criticize the Breach, Repair it!

> *'Thus says the Lord God, woe to the foolish prophets who are following their own spirit and have seen*

> *nothing. O Israel, your prophets have been like foxes among ruins. You have not gone up into the breaches, nor did you build the wall around the house of Israel to stand in the battle on the day of the Lord.'*
>
> (Ezekiel 13:3–5)

God needs people who, when they see a gap in the city-wide church wall, will go up into the breaches and rebuild the wall, so that the church will stand in the day of battle. In every city, town and village, you need the other churches if you are going to stand in the day of battle.

You may be thinking, 'You don't understand, I have revelation of the end-time move of God. These churches barely believe in Jesus.' The Word tells us that,

> '... *without any dispute, the lesser is blessed by the greater.'*
>
> (Hebrews 7:7)

If you are truly 'greater', you will seek ways to be a blessing to other churches. Your Christlike love will cast out fears. You will truly have a burden to see the entire body of Christ brought forth, not just your local assembly. In truth, Jesus said that the greatest among us would become the '... *servant of all*' (Mark 9:35; Matthew 23:11).

If a church in your city holds to and confesses Jesus, you need each other, and you must serve each other to complete God's work there. As you join one another for daily or weekly prayer, you will be surprised by God's preparation of others. Do not come with an attitude to teach or lead, but to love and serve. In this, God is not looking for leaders, but **followers** of the Lord Jesus Christ.

If we do not adjust to His will, we will be unable to stand against the enemy. Indeed, the day in which we live is not a day of peace, it is a time of war. God is gathering us together not only to Him and each other, but also against the spiritual forces of wickedness in every region. Therefore, the breaches between us must be filled, the walls built, and we must learn to stand together in the day of the Lord.

You Be the People

You do not have to go to college to find fault with the church. In fact, if you remember, you could find fault with the church even before you were a Christian. You do not need skill to find fault. But if you want to be like Christ, you have to die for people's sins. You have to be an intercessor who 'stands in the gap'. **The 'gap' is the distance between the way things are and the way things should be.** You stand in that space, cast down the accuser of the brethren and intercede! Have you seen something that is wrong? It is only because Jesus wants you to stand in the gap and see it changed. That is the only reason.

Some of us have cried for years, 'Where are the men to lead us into Christ's fullness?' We have assumed that God had others in mind for His purposes. What the Lord is saying, however, is **'You be the men and women that others are looking for.'** You be the peacemakers, the sons of God that bring healing and order to His church.

The responsibility is upon each of us. There is a tremendous job ahead, but the Lord Himself has promised,

> '...*those from among you will rebuild the ancient ruins; you will raise up the age-old foundations; and you will be called the repairer of the breach, the restorer of the paths in which to dwell.'* (Isaiah 58:12)

Let us lay our lives down in committed faith, that in our lifetimes, on this earth and in our communities, the corporate church of Jesus Christ will be restored, united and holy!

Chapter 13

God's Army of Worshippers

When the Scriptures refer to the 'Heavenly Host', we usually think of 'choirs of angels'. The word 'host' in the Bible meant 'army' (Luke 2:13). Let us perceive that the hosts of Heaven are worshipping armies. Indeed, no one can do warfare who is not first a worshipper of God.

The Central Issue in Tribulation: Worship

One does not have to penetrate deeply into the Revelation of John to discover that both God and the devil are seeking worshippers (Revelation 14:7; 7:11; 13:4; 14:11). Time and time again the line is drawn between those who *'worship the beast and his image'* and those who worship God.

Let us realize beforehand, that in the last great battle before Jesus returns, the outcome of every man's life shall be weighed upon a scale of worship: in the midst of warfare and battles, to whom will we bow, God or Satan?

Yet, while this warfare shall culminate in the establishment of the Lord's Kingdom on earth (Revelation 11:15), we must realize the **essence** of this battle is the central issue in our warfare today. Will we faithfully worship God during satanic assault and temptation? True worship must emerge now in the context of our daily lives, for no man will worship through the great battles of tomorrow who complains in the mere skirmishes of today.

You will remember that the Lord's call to the Israelites was a call to worship and service before Him in the wilderness (Exodus 5:3; 7:16). Indeed, when Moses first spoke of God's loving concern, we read that the Hebrews '... *bowed low and worshipped*' (Exodus 4:31). But when trials or pressures came, they fell quickly into murmuring, complaining and blatant rebellion. Their worship was superficial, a form without a heart of worship.

This same condition of shallow worship prevails in much of Christianity today. If a message is given that speaks of the Lord's great care for His people, with eagerness do we bow low and worship. But as soon as the pressures of daily living arise or temptations come, how quickly we rebel against God and resist His dealings! **The enemy has easy access to the soul that is not protected by true worship of God!** God's purpose in the wilderness was to perfect true worship, which is based upon the reality of God, not circumstances. The Lord knows that the heart that will worship Him in the wilderness of affliction will continue to worship in the promised land of plenty.

Without true worship of God, there can be no victory in warfare. **For what we bleed when we are wounded by satanic assault or difficult circumstances is the true measure of our worship.** You see, what comes out of our hearts during times of pressure was in us, but hidden, during times of ease. If you are a true worshipper, your spirit will exude worship to God no matter what battle you are fighting. In warfare, worship is a wall around the soul.

Protecting Your Heart Through Worship

Most of us understand the basic dynamics of the human soul. We have been taught, and rightly so, that the soul is the combination of our 'mind, will and emotions'. Generally speaking, when the enemy comes against the church, he targets any of these three areas. We must see that the protection of these areas is of vital importance in our war against Satan.

To further illuminate the nature of this battle, let us add something to our definition of the soul. Generally speaking, **the essence of who we are is made of events and how we responded to those events**. Who we are today is the sum of what we have encountered in life and our subsequent reactions. Abuses and afflictions hammer us one way, encouragement and praise inflates us another. Our reaction to each event, whether that event was positive or negative, is poured into the creative marrow of our individuality, where it is blended into the nature of our character.

What we call 'memory' is actually our spirit gazing at the substance of our soul. With few exceptions, **those events which we remember the most have shaped us the most**. Indeed, the reason our natural minds cannot forget certain incidents is because those experiences have literally become a part of our nature!

We are what the past has made us. Yet, we are commanded to '*...not look back*' and '*to forget ... those things which are behind*' (Philippians 3:13; Luke 9:62; Hebrews 11:15). With God, this is not impossible, for although the **events** of our lives are irreversible, our **reactions** to those events can still be changed. **And as our reactions change, we change.** In other words, although we cannot alter the past, we can put our past upon the 'altar' as an act of worship. A worshipping heart truly allows God to restore the soul.

All of us receive a portion of both good and evil in this world. But for life to be good, God, Who is the essence of life, must reach into our experiences and redeem us from our negative reactions. The channel through which the Lord extends Himself, even into our past, is our love and worship of Him.

> '*And we know that God causes all things to work together for good, for those who love God...*'
>
> (Romans 8:28a)

The key for the fulfilment of this verse is that we become lovers of God in our spirits. When we are given to loving

Him, all that we have passed through in life is washed in that love. It is redeemed and becomes good within us.

Therefore, it is essential to both the salvation of our souls and our protection in warfare that we be worshippers. For the ark which safely carries us through adversity is worship.

Psalm 84 expresses in praise to God the wonderful effect worship has upon the soul.

> *'How blessed is the man whose strength is in Thee; in whose heart are the highways to Zion! Passing through the valley of Baca* (weeping), *they make it a spring, the early rain also covers it with blessings.'*
>
> (Psalm 84:5–6)

If you are *'ever praising'* God (v. 4), your worship of God will transform the negative assault of the enemy into a spring of sweet waters which will refresh you. No matter what befalls a worshipper, their *'valley of weeping'* always becomes a spring covered with blessings. You cannot successfully engage in warfare, nor pass safely through the wilderness of this life, without first becoming a worshipper of God.

Worship: The Purpose of Creation

We were created for God's pleasure. We were not created to live for ourselves, but for Him. And while the Lord desires that we enjoy His gifts and His people, He would have us know we were created first for **His** pleasure. In these closing moments of this age, the Lord will have a people whose purpose for living is to please God with their lives. In them, God finds His own reward for creating man. They are His worshippers. They are on earth only to please God, and when He is pleased, they also are pleased. The Lord takes them farther and through more pain and conflicts than other men. Outwardly, they often seem *'smitten of God and afflicted'* (Isaiah 53:4). Yet to God, they are His beloved. When they are crushed, like the petals of a flower, they exude a worship, the fragrance of which is so beautiful and rare that angels weep in quiet awe at their surrender. They are the Lord's purpose for creation.

One would think that God would protect them, guarding them in such a way that they would not be marred. Instead, they are marred more than other men. Indeed, the Lord seems pleased to crush them, putting them to grief. For in the midst of their physical and emotional pain, their loyalty to Christ grows pure and perfect. And in the face of persecutions, their love and worship toward God becomes all-consuming.

Would that all Christ's servants were so perfectly surrendered. Yet God finds His pleasure in us all. But as the days of the Kingdom draw near and the warfare at the end of this age increases, those who have been created solely for the worship of God will come forth in the power and glory of the Son. With the high praises of God in their mouth, they will execute upon His enemies the judgment written (Psalm 149). They will lead as generals in the Lord's army of worshippers.

Chapter 14

Casting Down the Accuser of the Brethren

One may ask, 'How shall the Kingdom of God come and what sort of people shall possess it?' The Kingdom will be seen in a love-motivated people who know the power of prayer. For when they see a need, instead of judging one another, they intercede until they are built up into all aspects in Him Who is their head.

How the Kingdom Comes

> *'Now the salvation, and the power, and the Kingdom of our God and the authority of His Christ have come, for the accuser of our brethren has been thrown down, who accuses them before our God day and night.'*
>
> (Revelation 12:10–11)

There will be an actual point in time when the salvation, power and Kingdom of God, as well as the authority of Christ, is manifested in the earth. While we wait patiently for the fulfilment of that glorious event, the spirit of this eternal reality can be possessed any time a people determine to walk free of criticism and fault-finding, and turn their sights toward purity, love and prayer for each other.

There are God-ordained procedures to initiate correction within a church. These corrections should be done by *'you who are spiritual ... in a spirit of gentleness; looking to yourself, lest you too be tempted.'* Your motive should be to *'restore such a one'* (Galatians 6:1). Accusations against an elder, though, should not even be received except on the basis of two or three witnesses (1 Timothy 5:19). The 'witnesses' spoken of here are **eye**-witnesses, not the so-called 'spirit-witness' someone receives apart from hard and visible facts. All too often, these alleged 'witnesses' are sent by hell to destroy the harmony of a church with rumours and gossip.

When the scriptural approach to rectifying a situation is ignored, it opens the door to fault-finding, fleshly criticisms and judging, which are the evidences that the *'accuser of the brethren'* is assaulting the church. Where these sins are operative, the movement of the Holy Spirit is restricted: salvations are few, power is minimal and spiritual authority is crippled. Such a church is in serious danger.

To be truly anointed to bring Christ's corrections to a church, one must be anointed with Christ's motives. The Scriptures are plain, Jesus *'ever lives to make intercession for the saints'* (Romans 8:34; Hebrews 7:25). God does not call us to judge each other, but to pray for one another. If we see a need in the body of Christ, we must intercede and not simply criticize. Our pattern must be to follow Christ in building and restoring, not to echo the accuser of the brethren in finding fault.

Many years ago I belonged to a national Christian organization that had a true vision from God, yet also had several serious problems. At that time I was pastoring a small church and I felt perhaps we should leave this group because of what was wrong. Together, the congregation and I began to seek the Lord, with periods of fasting, for forty days. At the end of that time I wrote a 'list' of complaints and, holding them before God, I prayed (somewhat self-righteously), 'Lord, look at the errors in these people. Direct us, Lord, what should we do?'

Immediately the Lord replied, 'Have you seen these things?'

'Yes Lord,' I answered, 'I have seen their sins.'

To which He said, 'So also have I, but I died for them,

you go and do likewise.' From that day on, I found a grace from God to seek to be a source of life and prayer wherever I was serving God.

You see, we will always be serving in churches where things are wrong. Our response to what we see defines how Christlike we are actually becoming. If we see weakness in the body of Christ, our call is to supply strength. If we see sin, our response is to be an example of virtue. When we discover fear, we must impart courage, and where there is worldliness, we must display holiness. Our call is to enter the place of intercession and stand there until the body of Christ is built up in that area.

Is the Devil at the Throne of God?

Ephesians 2:6 tells us that we have been raised up and are seated *'with Christ in heavenly places'*. Let us understand that, while our bodies and souls are quite fixed here upon earth, through the agency of the Holy Spirit, our spirits have been brought into direct fellowship with Christ in Heaven. From this position, we can boldly approach God's throne of grace and we can enter through prayer and worship into the true holy place of God (Hebrews 4:16; 10:19–20; see also Matthew 5:8; Colossians 3:1–5).

There are many scriptures which support the truth of our positional seating with Christ. It is important for us to understand this, for we are going to examine a doctrine that has been a source of confusion for many saints: Is Satan in Heaven also? Is he actually standing before the throne of God?

Study the Book of Revelation and, in the description of God's throne, you will find no devil there (chapter 4). Investigate Hebrews, chapter twelve and, in the discourse concerning the Heavenly Jerusalem, again, you will see no devil in Heaven. To further emphasize this, during a home meeting in Toronto, Canada, while we were in deep worship before the Lord, in varying degrees the Holy Spirit opened to each of us a view into the Heavenly Jerusalem.

We saw a realm wherein there was neither darkness nor death. Everything was baptized in the living glory of God. There simply was no need of the sun nor of any other light, for everything was alive and within everything was the outraying light of God. We beheld many things, but my point is, there was no darkness nor any devil in Heaven.

Where then is Satan? Jude tells us that the devil and his demons are imprisoned, spiritually chained with *'eternal bonds...'* to *'...darkness reserved for judgment'* (Jude 6). Satan is **imprisoned** under darkness. The thought that the Heavenly Father, *...in Whom there is no darkness at all'* (1 John 1:5b), would countenance the devil intruding upon the eternal worship, accusing the very church for whom His Son had died, is unimaginable.

How then do we explain the scriptures which allude to a devil in Heaven? While we freely admit we do not know all the ways in which Satan accuses man before God, we do offer one solution. First, there are three realms known as 'heaven' in the Bible. The most commonly identified as such, is the eternal abode of God, angels and the redeemed. Next, the word 'heaven' is used to describe the sky; i.e., *...the heavens declare the glory of God'* (Psalm 19:1). But when the Bible says that Satan is in 'heaven' or the 'heavenly places' (Ephesians 6:12; Revelation 12:11; Luke 10:18), we believe it is with reference to the **spirit realm**.

This 'heaven', which immediately surrounds the consciousness of man, is the spiritual 'territory' from which Satan seeks to control the world. It would be foolish to assume we know more than we do about this dimension, but we know this: it is from here that Satan releases his war against the church.

If it is true that the devil is not in the highest heaven, how then does he accuse the saints **before the throne of God?** We began this discourse by explaining that Christ has positioned our spirits in Him before God's throne. While our spirits connect us to God, our bodies and souls are here on earth. Although the devil does not have immediate access to God, he does have access to our **thoughts** and **words**. When we harbor sympathetic attitudes toward fault-finding, when we justify gossip and negative criticism, we are actually giving Satan the use of our mouths to accuse the saints before God!

We have wrongly assumed that our whispers, spoken in darkness, remained hidden even from God. We must realize that

> *'all things are open and laid bare to the eyes of Him with whom we have to do.'* (Hebrews 4:13)

Is it not written, *'. . . what you have said in the darkness shall be heard in the light.'* (Luke 12:3)? God, Who is Light, indeed hears the voice of the accuser, even in the guarded confidences spoken to a spouse.

Guard Your Tongue!

Much of what the Father supplies to the body of Christ is furnished through our confession. This is not simply our positive, premeditated confession expressed in prayer; it consists of everything that comes out of our mouths. Did not Christ Himself say men shall be judged for *'every idle* (or careless) *word that they speak'* (Matthew 12:36)?

Our words are the overflow of the condition of our hearts. Christ, as the *'High Priest of our confession'* (Hebrews 3:1), takes our words, whether in faith or unbelief, and allocates back to us eternal life in proportion to our words. When our tongue is unbridled, James tells us that our negative confession

> *'. . . sets on fire the course of our life, and is set on fire by hell.'* (James 3:6)

If we are supportive of one another, loving one another, protecting one another, we experience much growth and greater protection. If, however, we are finding fault, criticizing and talebearing, the voice of the accuser is manifested, and we are judged for our idle and evil words. God looks at what we have said and gives us reality accordingly.

Consequently, we must come to understand that each of our thoughts, and even our most intimate conversations with men, are prayers we are offering to the Father, who sees all things continually and in secret. These unaddressed prayers are just as much a part of our confession as our 'Dear Lord' prayers, and they are just as influential. Our words about one another, as well as our words to one another, should carry with them the same sense of reverence as when we speak with God. For He is, indeed, listening.

Other Tongues or *Flaming* Tongues?

It is significant that when Isaiah saw the Lord (Isaiah 6), not only was there no devil in Heaven, but the guilt he felt was due to his **words**. He said,

> '... Woe is me, for I am ruined! Because I am a man of **unclean lips**, and I live among a people of **unclean lips**.'
> (Isaiah 6:5)

The fact is, our criticisms of one another are the voice of Satan accusing the saints before God.

Isaiah's lips were cleansed as they were touched by a burning coal, taken from the altar of God. The closer we truly draw to God, the more guilt we shall feel for our unclean words. When the Holy Spirit was manifested upon Jesus, He came symbolically in the form of a dove. But when the Spirit was revealed at Pentecost, He appeared as flaming tongues of fire. Certain segments of Christianity have made speaking in 'other tongues' a sign of the infilling of the Holy Spirit. For us, the issue shall not be speaking in foreign tongues, but **flaming** tongues; tongues which have been purified by the fire of God from the altar, tongues that are cleansed of fault-finding and criticisms.

Casting Down the Accuser

> '*And they overcame him because of the blood of the Lamb and . . . the word of their testimony, and they did not love their own lives, even unto death.*'
>
> (Revelation 12:10–11)

Instead of talking about people's sins and faults, we must ask God for the grace to see our common needs met. Instinctively, we must enter into the intercession of Christ and passionately intercede for those for whom Jesus died. In Revelation 12, we see how they overcame the accuser of the brethren.

Let us look at each dimension of our victory separately.

1. ***The Blood of the Lamb:*** One blood spiritually flows through us all, literally making us one body, sharing one Source of cleansing and one Source of life. One blood makes us family: blood bought and blood relatives. The blood pays for our redemption and in the attack of the accuser, disarms his accusations. The blood establishes us in an attitude of meekness rather than self-righteousness, for the shedding of the blood declares our common need of Jesus.

2. ***The Word of their Testimony:*** This includes telling others what God has done for you, but it is more. The '*. . . testimony of Jesus is the spirit of prophecy*' (Revelation 19:10). To truly overcome the enemy we must live and think prophetically. That is, we must see each other as God sees us, seeing the 'end from the beginning', animated by lives of vision, confessing our faith for one another. Knowing and speaking the Living Word of God enables us to overcome the illusions of the enemy (1 Timothy 1:18).

3. ***Loving not our own Lives, even unto Death:*** We cannot overcome Satan and simultaneously harbor self-pity and sympathy for that which needs to be crucified within us. Our victory is consummated by our willingness to go even to death rather than betray our convictions of truth. Paul said, '*. . . I do not consider my life of*

any account as dear to myself that I may finish my course... ' (Acts 20:24). Those who establish the Kingdom are uncompromising with their own 'hurts'. They may ache, but not withdraw. They live by faith.

The accuser must be cast down first **in our minds!** We cannot tolerate fault-finding and accusations. We must possess the very heart of God toward our brethren. The Kingdom of God and the authority of His Christ will be seen in a people who are terminally committed to love-motivated prayer. For when they see a need, instead of becoming critical, they cast down the accuser of the brethren, and they pray!

PART THREE:

The Battleground
of the Heavenly Places

The last frontier of battle is the heavenly places, the dimension known today as the spirit realm. It is here that angels and demons wage their war for our cities. But let the reader take note: this dimension is currently enemy territory! Only according to the measure that our heart is like Christ's do we have authority in the heavenlies; only a city-wide, Christ-centered church can displace the powers of darkness from the spirit realm.

Note: It would be helpful to read the Glossary at the end of the book for clarity and definition concerning the chapters in the next two sections.

Chapter 15

The War Over Reality

**Created in the image of God, man was given limited,
yet distinct, inherent powers. He was granted the power
to imagine, as well as the faculty to define and then
establish reality. And, operating within the boundaries
preset by God, man does this, for better or worse,
according to the free selection of his will. As we understand this, we see that the essence of spiritual warfare is
in who shall define reality: the Word of God or the
illusions of this present age.**

What We Agree Upon

What is reality? How does life appear – to you? The dictionary defines reality as '... that which is real; an actual
thing, situation or event'. Such is reality in terms of objective analysis. But reality is not just objective, there is also a
subjective or personal side to reality which is rooted in our
feelings, attitudes and beliefs. From this perspective, life is
'... *done to* [us] *as* [we] *have believed*' (Matthew 8:13).

In this personal side of reality, what seems real to one is
very often unreal to another. Consider the Eskimo's view
of reality: traveling by dog sled and dwelling in an igloo,
living in the land of the northern lights and the midnight
sun. Compare that to a businessman living in New York
City: traveling in subways and automobiles, living in a
concrete world of skyscrapers and parking lots; with the

stress of rush hours and a high-pressure job in a brokerage firm. Reality in both locations, though strikingly different, is uniquely functional and subjectively real to each individual.

Let us, therefore, learn from these examples an important principle: **whatever a society agrees upon and establishes through consent, compromise and constant use will ultimately define reality to them.** Understanding this precept is very important because, as we come into agreement with the principles and standards of the Kingdom of God, our whole definition of society is going to change.

An example of this in Scripture is seen in the book of Genesis.

> *'And the Lord said, "Behold, they are one people, and they have all one language; and this is only the beginning of what they will do; and now nothing they have imagined they can do will be impossible to them."'*
>
> (Genesis 11:6 Amplfied)

This is what the Lord Himself said concerning the ungodly Babylonians. He said that whatever mankind imagined, it had the potential to accomplish. If you doubt the validity of that statement, you would have stood among the scoffers when dreamers envisioned themselves standing on the moon. You would have scorned the concept that voices and images could be transmitted around the world through invisible frequencies. You would have ridiculed the idea that weapons would become powerful enough to destroy all life on earth. Yet, today these things are part of our world because of man's power to establish reality. If a man's mind can imagine it and he can get others to believe in it, their spirits can accomplish it. And with few exceptions, nothing will be impossible, even for as small a group as two or three, once they believe a thing can happen.

This is exactly what the warfare is centered upon in the church today: the devil wants us to accept Christianity **as it is**, as though division, sin and spiritual impotency were the ultimate reality God has provided for believers on earth. Satan wants us to **agree with and thereby reinforce** this deceptive view of the church. There are many promises which are yet to be fulfilled concerning the people of God: holy and noble purposes which shall unfold in the last days. Therefore, our agreement must be with **God's plan** for a holy, undivided, powerful church, for He is calling us to establish **His** kingdom, not the status quo! While we must work with the church as it is, we must ever realize that what we see in Christianity is **not** what the church will be like before Jesus returns! In fact, our call is to cooperate with God in the bringing forth of revival and the raising up of the body of Christ.

> '*That He might present to Himself the church in all her glory, having no spot or wrinkle or any such thing; but that she should be holy and blameless.*'
>
> (Ephesians 5:27)

Before Jesus returns, the Father has promised His Son a bride without spot or wrinkle. She shall be a powerful witness of Christ Himself in the earth.

War in Heaven: The Principle of Displacement

> '*Then war broke out in heaven, Michael and his angels going forth to battle with the dragon; and the dragon and his angels fought, but they were defeated and there was no room found for them in heaven any longer.*'
>
> (Revelation 12:7–8 Amplified)

Notice the phrase, '*there was no room ... for them in heaven*'. The war against principalities involves displacement: Christ filling the spiritual territories once held by Satan.

This event is difficult for us to comprehend. How do angels and demons, beings who do not die from wounds, wage war? With what do they do battle? And how do they conquer one another? Without exceeding the bounds of our knowledge, we can safely say this: **All spiritual warfare is waged over one essential question. Who will control reality on earth; Heaven or hell?**

When it comes to angelic and demonic warfare, the battle rests not in physical weaponry, but in the **power of agreement** between mankind and the spirit realm. We read in Ephesians 6 that '...*principalities and powers*' occupy the *'heavenly places'* (v. 12). But we read in Ephesians 1:10 that it is the Father's expressed purpose to sum up all things in Christ, '...*things in the heavens and things upon the earth.*' Ephesians 3:10 reveals God's glorious plan, '...*that through the church*' God has purposed to make known His manifold wisdom '...*unto the principalities and powers in the heavenly places!*' You see, as the body of Christ on earth agrees with its Head in Heaven, the Spirit of Christ Himself displaces the powers of darkness in the heavenly places.

In other words, when the church on earth is aggressive in its agreement with the Will and Word of God, then the Presence of God increases in the spiritual realm, proportionally displacing the influence of hell on earth. Shortly thereafter, manifesting in the world of men, we see revivals, healings and miracles. But when the church is passive, indifferent or carnal, the powers of hell increase their rule over the affairs of men: marriages break up, crime increases and wantonness becomes unbridled. We must see that our prayers, attitudes and agreement with God are an integral part of establishing the reality of the Kingdom of God on earth!

The Devil is a Liar

Satan is unmasked in Scripture as *'a liar, and the father of lies'* (John 8:44). His realm of operation is the spirit world that immediately surrounds and blankets the consciousness of mankind. This realm is known as the 'heavenly places' in the Bible (Ephesians 6:12). From this spiritual realm Satan works to corrupt and control the mind of man through illusions built from mankind's carnal desires and fears. But the power of the lie is not merely the speaking of false-hoods, nor is it that this world is an illusion. The lie of the enemy appears most powerfully when men believe that this world, **as it is**, is the only world we can live in. The truth is, of course, that God is establishing His Kingdom, and ultimately every other reality will submit to and be ruled by that Kingdom! (Hebrews 12:26–28; Revelation 11:15).

The weapon God has given us to combat the lies of the enemy is the Word of God, which the Scriptures refer to as the *'sword of the Spirit'* (Ephesians 6:17). Jesus said His words *'. . . are spirit and are life'* (John 6:63), which is to say that the substance, or meaning, in Christ's words represents an actual reality: the living Spirit of the Kingdom of God.

We should also recognize that the ancient Greeks, in whose language the New Testament was written, had no word for 'reality'. To them 'truth' and 'reality' were the same essence. When we think of the *'Spirit of Truth'* we must include in our understanding the concept of **reality**; that is, the Holy Spirit and the Word of God is **reality itself!**

This point is essential: in our war over who controls man's world, the singular weapon God has given the church is His Spirit-empowered Word. The Living Word of the Spirit is the truth. Paul taught that spiritual warfare deals specifically with the *'pulling down of strongholds'*. But what are those strongholds? They are **lies** the devil has sown into our thought processes which, as we accepted and believed them, became reality to us. We do not **fall** in sin as much as we are **seduced** by it; every sin is cloaked in some measure of deception. But, as these lies are uncovered and destroyed, as our thought-processes are freed from illu-sions, we will discover the blamelessness, perfection and truth of Christ in us, the hope of glory (Colossians 1:27).

Standing Upon the Word of God

To be successful in battle, we must know the Word of God. If you are in need of deliverance, or if you are being used in the ministry of deliverance, the following verses will be helpful in establishing victory. It is not wise to engage in any kind of spiritual warfare without knowing these scriptures perfectly from memory.

> *'For the weapons of our warfare are not carnal, but mighty through God to the pulling down of strongholds. We are destroying speculations and every lofty thing raised up against the knowledge of God, and we are taking every thought captive to the obedience of Christ.'* (2 Corinthians 10:4–5)

> *'And do not participate in the unfruitful deeds of darkness, but instead even expose them...'*
> (Ephesians 5:8–13)

When you expose and confess your sins, they no longer are in darkness (secrecy). When light is turned on in a dark room, darkness becomes light. So also, when you bring your sins out of darkness and expose them to light, they vanish in God's forgiveness; they become light.

> *'If we confess our sins, He is faithful and righteous to forgive us our sins and to cleanse us from all unrighteousness.'* (1 John 1:9)

Again, confess your sins. God is faithful and just to forgive *and to cleanse* you of *all* unrighteousness.

> *'But thanks be to God, who always leads us in His triumph in Christ, and manifests through us the sweet aroma of the knowledge of Him in every place.'*
> (2 Corinthians 2:14)

There is victory, right here, right now because Christ is in you.

> *'For God has not given us a spirit of fear, but of power and love and a sound mind.'* (2 Timothy 1:7)

Do not fear Satan's threats. Always remember, the devil is 'a liar and truth is not in him'.

> '...*through death He might render powerless him who had the power of death, that is, the devil; and might deliver those who through fear of death were subject to slavery all their lives.*' (Hebrews 2:14–15)

Satan may try to make you believe he has power over you, but Jesus says that Satan has been 'rendered powerless' in our lives. Use the Name of Jesus and the Word of God to break the power of Satan's lies.

> '*And we know that God causes all things to work together for good to those who love God, to those who are called according to His purpose.*' (Romans 8:28–29)

If God causes everything to work for good as you love Him, then ultimately, nothing bad can ever happen to you. God has predestined you to be conformed to the image of His Son.

> '*Behold, I have given you authority to tread upon serpents and scorpions, and over all the power of the enemy, and nothing shall injure you.*' (Luke 10:19)

Jesus has given us authority over **all** of Satan's power. We have His authority and His promise that nothing shall injure us!

> '*The Son of God appeared for this purpose, that He might destroy the works of the devil.*' (1 John 3:8b)

You have been set free – not because you 'feel' free, but because you have faith. Each time you speak your faith, you are **establishing** your freedom as a true reality. Your confidence is that while you are praying, the angelic hosts of God, which outnumber the devil by at least two to one, are united with you against evil. With Jesus, you cannot fail!

(See also Isaiah 42:13; 53; 54:11–17; Romans 10:8–9; Ephesians 6:18; James 4:7.)

Chapter 16

Exposing the Spirit of Antichrist!

There is an order of beings whose iron fist rules the empire of hell; their cloud of evil darkens nearly every facet of life on earth. To topple this wicked kingdom and prevail victoriously in our warfare, we must discern our enemies and set to flight these commanders of darkness.

More Than Just a Man

There exists a ruler of darkness, a principality of the deadliest order, that has been tolerated by believers for so long that its influence is considered **normal** for the church. This diabolical entity is the spirit of Antichrist. While this spirit manifests itself wherever true Christianity is openly persecuted, it is a demon whose nature is primarily religious. This spirit stands firmly in opposition against the unfolding restoration of the church of Jesus Christ.

As this demon's name is, so is he. He is simply 'anti' or against Christ. This principality uses the power-demons of Jealousy, Fear, Unforgiveness and Ambition – whatever is necessary to keep independent, local churches from becoming the 'armed and dangerous', **united** body of Christ.

It is easy to lock our interpretation of the 'Antichrist' into a particular personage who will be revealed just prior to Christ's return. Indeed, most Christians are in agreement that such a man will ultimately emerge. This individual will

> '...oppose and exalt himself above every god or object
> of worship, so that he takes his seat in the temple of
> God, displaying himself as being God.'
>
> (2 Thessalonians 2:4)

But, if this is Antichrist in his human, manifested form,
then this also describes the nature or essence of the Antichrist spirit in its invisible form.

This spirit of Antichrist has been prevalent in the church
since the first century. In fact, the Apostle John plainly
states that there were *'many antichrists'* in the first century.
He wrote,

> *'Children, it is the last hour; and just as you heard that
> Antichrist is coming, even now many antichrists have
> arisen...'* (1 John 2:18)

When we compare this verse with 2 Thessalonians 2:4, we
see that our understanding of the term 'antichrist' has been
too narrow when limited to one man in the future. John
said, *'...even now **many** antichrists have arisen'* (1 John
2:18).

It is important to grasp that John is actually speaking of
people who once seemed to be members of the united, city-
wide Christian community. The apostle tells us that they
'...went out from us.' He said *'...if they had been of us,
they would have remained with us'* (1 John 2:19).

What motivated these misled souls? Later in John's epis-
tle, the apostle reveals it was the Antichrist spirit. He wrote
in chapter four,

> *'...every spirit that does not confess Jesus is not from
> God; and this is the spirit of the Antichrist, of which you
> have heard that it is coming, and now it is already in the
> world...'* (1 John 4:3)

John makes a distinct reference here to the **spirit of Antichrist**, which he stated was already in the world.

John identifies this spirit as one which does not confess Jesus. To a first-century saint, to *'confess Jesus'* meant more than simply mentioning His name after a prayer. Essentially, it was to speak from a state of oneness with Him, enabling His actual Spirit to be manifested (see Matthew 10:32 Amplified). They confessed the **Person** Jesus, not just the name 'Jesus'! Christ Himself was revealed through their attitudes of love, commitment and sacrifice!

In the next verse John explained the nature of the Antichrist spirit.

> *'... By this we know the spirit of truth and the spirit of error. Beloved, **let us love one another**, for love is from God; and everyone who loves is born of God and knows God. The one who does not love does not know God, for God is love.'* (1 John 4:6b–8)

We discern the spirit of truth from the spirit of error – or more specifically, the Spirit of Christ from the spirit of Antichrist – by the measure of Christ's **love** operating in an individual or church. John says that, *'the one who does not love does not know God.'* **An individual or church that thinks God is pleased with them, yet they do not walk in love, may actually be serving the spirit of Antichrist!** Christians are to be known *'... by their love,'* not merely their theology (John 13:35)! When John wrote of truth and error, he spoke specifically of the Antichrist spirit and our openness to this spirit through loveless church attitudes!

This display of the Antichrist is far more subtle and much more subversive than what may take place when the *'man of sin'* is openly revealed. The Antichrist spirit hardens the heart, keeping it from love. It nurtures unforgiving attitudes, causing those under its influence to splinter from a church due to various criticisms and minor doctrinal differences. It is the 'strong man' behind most church splits.

Following Christ, however, calls us to embrace forgiveness and love as a way of life. It is simply 'anti' Christ to justify unforgiveness, division and selfish ambition. **The**

Antichrist spirit will be disguised behind any number of issues, but those issues are simply tools this principality uses to divide the church.

The spirit of Antichrist is simply that spirit which is anti-Christ! It is anti-love, anti-forgiveness, anti-reconciliation! Perhaps more than all others, this principality keeps good churches divided from one another.

Antichrist is the true source of numerous church splits. Indeed, if you pray against this spirit instead of what seems like the immediate issues, many church splits would be averted. In this sense, we must guard very carefully how strongly we cling to our ideas and criticisms. For if our thoughts exalt themselves above God's ability to correct us, we will certainly become a target for the spirit of Antichrist.

Remember, the Antichrist spirit may use jealousy or fear or even the color of the church bathrooms as a smoke-screen, but the essential cause of most division is simply Christians yielding to someone or something other than the Spirit and teachings of Jesus Christ. Any situation can be reconciled by returning to the words of Jesus. Once all parties agree to yield to Him, love and victory soon follow.

Deliverance from Antichrist on a Personal Level

Each of us has thinking processes, strongholds in our minds, which have been shaped and conditioned by the spirit of Antichrist. Let us not defend those thoughts which are 'anti' Christ; rather let us expose them as sin and see them defeated. Antichrist has been around for a long time; its thought-systems may not depart suddenly from any of us. But if we can discern the difference between the loving voice of Christ and the arrogant rebellion of Antichrist, we can take a major step toward seeing our lives conformed to Christ.

How do you know if the lack of love you feel toward other churches is only your flesh or if it is a stronghold for the spirit of Antichrist? Repent for rebellion. Then audibly pray against the Antichrist spirit. You will immediately discover a distance between you and the enemy and a closeness between you and the Lord.

Christianity Without the Antichrist Influence

There are many ways the Antichrist spirit seeks to display itself as being God, i.e., the New Age Movement, Communism, etc. But the unique way it masquerades as **God in the Church** is this: there is a natural, religious reverence men have toward death. Antichrist uses this phenomenon by conditioning congregations to accept the solemnity of death as though it were true reverence of God. The Almighty is not the God of the dead, but of the living, and true reverence is that which is accompanied by awe, joy and thanksgiving. You can discern Antichrist in a congregation that is reverent toward its deadness. The atmosphere is not filled with holiness, but hollowness. **It is the same essence that lingers in an empty funeral home.** Antichrist will sit over a people, exuding an aura of coldness that literally fills the atmosphere of a church building.

When the Holy Spirit first began to reveal this entity to us, we saw how it had distorted our basic concept of Christianity. In fact, the stronghold of antichrist thinking is an 'acceptable' condition in the church. This spirit has so worked its way into '...*the temple of God*' (the corporate, but divided city-church), that in many congregations and to many believers, '*it displays ... itself as being God*' (2 Thessalonians 2:4).

It was obvious to us that this principality was seeking to '*exalt ... itself above everything that is called God.*' When we sought to teach the people, the words of our message fell to the ground amidst tremendous resistance, as though a blanket were covering them. We sought the Lord and a few days later upon awakening, the Holy Spirit revealed the discernment we had been missing. He illuminated the first words of 2 Thessalonians 2:4, '*he opposes.*'

The Antichrist spirit literally **opposes** truth, especially new truth that reveals its nature. It resists any movement in the body of Christ toward life. In the churches where it presides, should an 'amen' squeak out of one in support of the preaching, this spirit glares through the faces of those whose minds are its stronghold.

When we better understood the Antichrist spirit, we could war successfully against it. Our intercessors began to pray against this spirit's influence over our county. Less than one week later, five other pastors and myself, as well as several para-church ministries, gathered together and committed ourselves to meet for weekly intercessory prayer in each other's churches. Three months later, that number had doubled and has been increasing ever since. How did it occur? The intercessors discerned and bound the spirit of Antichrist. Suddenly the godly desires to meet and pray with other pastors began to prevail in our community!

Understanding the City-Wide Church

God sees the church community as one body fused together in the fire of Christ's love. He would have us praying together, working and building our churches in the Spirit of His Kingdom. No one knows the local battle better than the local pastors. When Jesus spoke to the churches in the Revelation of John, He spoke to them as individual churches with battles unique to their separate regions. He did not say, 'To such-and-such church, whose headquarters is in London.' No. These were local men who knew the people's needs, and Jesus viewed them as such.

The pastors were united in one front against the enemy. They were accountable both to God and each other; a true plurality of leadership in each community. The city-wide church, as God sees it, would be free from jealousy, 'sheep stealing' and personal ambition. It would truly be one body.

Yet, Antichrist's penetration into typical Christian thinking is so deep that its deceptions are preached from pulpits and accepted in the pews. Therefore, you must persevere for the sake of Christ in your community. Let your faith be large, but your fleshly ambitions small. Personal ambition is the motive of the Antichrist; it is the name of the stronghold that has made us divided. You must not approach others with personal ambitions, but as their servant. If you are called to a leadership role, the others will recognize that call by your meekness and good fruit. Your ministry will come naturally, without self-promotion. Remember the commandment of Jesus:

> *'Do not be called leaders; for One is your Leader, that is Christ.'*   (Matthew 23:10)

In truth, God is not raising up leaders; He is training servant-followers, men and women who will pray together for Christ's leading.

Therefore, when you meet with Christians from other churches, come as their servants and look to bless them. If you are a pastor, find out the needs of your fellow pastors and begin to pray for them. Perhaps one needs a piano player; if you have two, send a pianist (Luke 3:11). Most pastors struggle with unique fears and insecurities. But if you come in the love of God, you will disarm his fears.

The spirit of Antichrist is a *'world-ruler'* (Ephesians 6:12). It cannot be cast out as a lesser demon might. Ultimate victory over all such principalities comes through **displacement**, where the encouragement and love of Christ floods the thought-life of the local Christian community. As we become the opposite of Antichrist, we will see Christ's body healed, and the spirit of Antichrist trodden under our feet.

Chapter 17

Discerning the Spirit of Jezebel

We are going to confront a stronghold of immense proportions. It is a way of thinking that exists unchecked in most churches. We are going to expose and then destroy the hiding places of Jezebel.

Understanding the Spirit of Jezebel

> *'But I have this against you, that you tolerate the woman Jezebel, who calls herself a prophetess, and she teaches and leads my bond-servants astray, so that they commit acts of immorality and eat things sacrificed to idols.*
>
> (Revelation 2:20)

You may challenge my using the above quote and addressing it to American churches. You may argue that not one of the pastors you know has anyone who openly instructs people to commit acts of immorality. I understand your sense of alarm. I agree that you probably know of no one who brazenly preaches that sexual lust and idolatry are not sins. When we speak of Jezebel, we are identifying the source in our society of obsessive sensuality, unbridled witchcraft and hatred for male authority.

To understand the spirit of Jezebel, we must understand the genesis of this personality in the Bible. The first mention of Jezebel is seen in the rebellious, manipulative wife of King Ahab. It was actually this spirit, operating through Queen Jezebel, which had caused over ten million Hebrews – all but seven thousand faithful souls – to bow to Baal and '... *forsake the covenant, destroy the sacred altars ... and kill the prophets'* (1 Kings 19:14–18). This one spirit was nearly totally responsible for corrupting an entire nation, and this principality has come full force against our nation.

Jezebel is fiercely independent and intensely ambitious for pre-eminence and control. It is noteworthy that the name 'Jezebel', literally translated, means 'without cohabitation'. This simply means she refuses 'to live together' or 'co-habit' with anyone. Jezebel will not dwell with anyone unless she can control and dominate the relationship. When she seems submissive or 'servant-like', it is only for the sake of gaining some strategic advantage. From her heart, she yields to no one.

Bear in mind that the spirit which produced Jezebel existed before its namesake was born. Although we refer to Jezebel as 'she', this spirit is without gender. However, it is important to note that, while men in leadership are the main targets of most principalities, Jezebel is more attracted to the uniqueness of the female psyche in its sophisticated ability to manipulate without physical force.

Look for Jezebel to target women who are embittered against men, either through neglect or misuse of authority. This spirit operates through women who, because of insecurity, jealousy or vanity, desire to control and dominate others. Jezebel is there behind the woman who publicly humiliates her husband with her tongue, and then thereafter controls him by his fear of public embarrassment.

While she uses every means of sexual perversity known in hell, immorality is not the issue; **control** is what she seeks, using the power of sexual passions for the purpose of possessing men. To a woman under the influence of Jezebel, 'conquering' a man need not involve physical contact if a seductive glance of her eyes will capture him.

The Battle Has Expanded

Since the era of the early apostles, and especially since the dawn of the electronic age, the scale of battle has greatly enlarged. It is difficult for us in our generation to discern the scope of warfare that hits the church and the world in general. We might actually suppose that warfare should decrease since the number of demons has not changed since the first century, while mankind has grown from three hundred million to over five billion souls today. Yet, the **access** the devil has to the souls in our world has increased through the mass communications media and literature. John wrote of this period in time in Revelation 12:15.

> '*And the serpent poured water like a river out of his mouth after the woman, so that he might cause her* [the church] *to be swept away with the flood.*'
>
> (Revelation 12:15)

Water, in this context, symbolizes 'words'. In our world there exists a flood of **words** and **visual images** coming out of the mouth of Satan. Our society, through technological advances, has made sins of the mind and heart more accessible. More than ever before, the carnal mind, with its openness to this satanic flood of filth and rebellion, is being structured into a powerful stronghold for the devil.

In our information-filled, entertainment-oriented world, even minor demons can exercise major influence simply by possessing the script writers and producers of movies and television. Indeed, Satan has always been '. . . *the prince of the power of the air*' (Ephesians 2:2). But we should realize that the '*power of the air*' is not merely the wind; we see that in our world this power uniquely includes the electronic airwaves which carry radio and television signals.

Therefore, we must discern exactly where the satanic inroads are in our own lives and cut them off. We cannot worship God Sunday morning and then tolerate Jezebel through immoral entertainment in a movie Sunday night. Indeed, it is with this in mind that, in regard to warring against Jezebel, the Eternal Word specifically described Himself as *. . . He who searches the **minds** and **hearts**'* (Revelation 2:23), for it is in the inner sanctuary of our private soul-life where tolerance to Jezebel begins. It is here, within us, where tolerance must end.

Set the Captives Free!

Jezebel's spirit flows unhindered throughout the entertainment industries. It flaunts itself in the world of fashion; it holds degrees in the philosophical departments of our schools and colleges. Where can you go in our society that the influence of this spirit is not felt? She is the destroyer of politician and preacher alike. She is the cruel motivator behind abortion. It is Jezebel who generates dissatisfaction between spouses.

This spirit was sitting in the church in Thyatira when the Holy Spirit exposed it nineteen hundred years ago (Revelation 2:19–29). It still has its favorite seat in church. There are respectable men who love God and who seek to serve Him, yet secretly in their hearts they are prisoners of Jezebel. Even now, they are deeply ashamed of their bondage to pornography; and they can barely control their desires for women. Ask them to pray and their spirits are awash with guilt and shame. Their prayers are but the whimpers of Jezebel's eunuchs.

There are good women who come to church seeking God, but this spirit has them fantasizing about the men in the assembly; lamenting that their husbands are not as 'spiritual' as other husbands. Soon, these women develop problems that 'only the pastor' can understand. Ladies, the *'older women'* – the **godly** women in the church – are the ones you need to consult with first, not pastor or elders (Titus 2:3–5). If you must counsel with a church leader, do not be offended when he asks for his wife or an older, godly woman to join him.

Anyone who is hit by this spirit needs, first of all, to repent deeply of their sympathetic thoughts toward it, and then **war** against it! Do not waste days and weeks under condemnation. Separate yourself from that Jezebelian thinking which was fostered upon you in your youth, pick up the sword of the Spirit and war against the principality of Jezebel! Pray for the saints in your church. Pray for the Christians throughout your community. **If you war against Jezebel when you are tempted, eventually you are going to become dangerous!** This spirit will stop attacking you once it recognizes that your aggressive counterattack is setting other people free!

Likely Targets

As we identify those whom this spirit is most likely to influence, let us recognize that this demon can also operate through men. In fact, Jezebel seeks the highly refined qualities of the professional musician, especially when such a man has both the ambition and the opportunity to become a worship leader or director. It will also seek to surface in the life of the pastor himself, in which case he will become very authoritarian and unyielding in his control of the church. Such a pastor will invariably be isolated from fellowship and accountability with other pastors. The man will find himself lured into maintaining flirtatious and sensual relationships, 'special intimacies' with one or more women in the church. In time, he will most likely succumb to adultery.

Yet this spirit prefers the disposition of a woman's nature. And since certain female ministries are more involved than others, it follows that they would be targets for the spirit of Jezebel. Church leaders should take heed. This spirit will seek to manoeuvre itself into leadership positions. Remember, Jesus said of Jezebel, '... [she] *calls herself a prophetess*' (Revelation 2:20). A woman can most certainly function prophetically; she can be anointed by God to serve in delegated authority as a prophetess. But when she insists upon recognition, when she manipulates or entirely disregards the male leadership in the church, **when she *'calls herself a prophetess'*,** beware.

Prayer leaders, church secretaries, worship and song leaders, pastors and their wives, you are all especially targeted by this spirit. All of you serving in these roles should be instructed and warned about the warfare that may come against you. Each of you should be part of a church 'warfare team' that is trained to war against Jezebel.

What Jezebel Hates

Jezebel's worst enemies are the prophets; her worst fear is that the people will embrace repentance. Jezebel hates repentance. Though this spirit will infiltrate the church, masking its desire for control with true Christian doctrines, it will hide from true repentance.

Jezebel hates humility. Jesus taught that greatness in the kingdom was measured in childlike honesty of heart, not in what we appear to be to others. **A true ministry is willing and eager to be submitted and accountable to other ministries.** It is typical of those who are servant-minded. Therefore, we must learn that spirituality is measured in meekness, not power.

Jezebel hates prayer. Intercessory prayer pries her fingers off the hearts and souls of men. It sets people free in the spirit. When you pray, it binds her. When you pray against immorality, it cripples her. When you pray for a submissive heart, it is like the trampling of Jehu's horse upon her body.

Jezebel hates the prophets, for the prophets speak out against her. The prophets are her worst enemies. When she wars, it is to stir people against the message of the prophetic church. More than she hates the prophets, she hates the Word they speak. Her real enemy is the spoken Word of God.

Jezebel's ultimate hatred is against God Himself. She hates the grace God lavishes upon His bondservants, even after they sin. She hates the fact that God will take the weakest and lowliest and use them to bring her down. She hates the holiness and purity of heart that comes from God and surrounds those who serve in His courts.

Let's pray:

'Father, we submit to You and Your standard of right-eousness. We ask for purity, meekness and holiness of heart. Forgive us for our tolerance of the spirit of Jezebel in both our mind and our deeds.

Father, because we submit to You, we have Your authority to resist the devil. We bind, in the name of Jesus, the principality of Jezebel. We pull down the stronghold of its thinking over our community and our state. We come against the fortresses this demon has built up in the spirit realm in this area and we release the Holy Spirit to plunder the house of Jezebel and distribute her goods.

We also speak faithfulness of eyes and heart to hus-bands and wives. We release purity of heart and grace to each member of the body of Christ, both single and married. We cover Your people with the blood of Jesus. We loose the joy of a humble and submissive spirit and pull down the imaginations of ambition and pride. In Jesus' Name. Amen!'

Chapter 18

Elijah, Jehu and the War Against Jezebel

There is a war, a very ancient war, between the spirit of Elijah and the spirit of Jezebel. In this age-old battle, Elijah represents the interests of Heaven: the call to repentance and the return to God. Jezebel, on the other hand, represents that unique principality whose purpose is to hinder and defeat the work of repentance.

To the Victor Goes Our Nation

To understand the conflict between the Elijah spirit and the spirit of Jezebel, we must understand these two adversaries as they are seen in the Scriptures. Each is the spiritual counterpart of the other. Is Elijah bold? Jezebel is brazen. Is Elijah ruthless toward evil? Jezebel is vicious toward righteousness. Does Elijah speak of the ways and words of God? Jezebel is full of systems of witchcraft and words of deceit. The war between Elijah and Jezebel continues today. The chief warriors on either side are the prophets of both foes; to the victor goes the soul of our nation.

In the tradition of Samuel, Elijah was the head of the school of prophets. Under him were the sons of the prophets – literally hundreds of seers and prophetic minstrels – who proclaimed the word of the Lord. In this war, however, Jezebel had viciously and systematically murdered all of God's servants until only Elijah remained (1 Kings 18:22). Elijah, as the last of the prophets, then challenged the 450 prophets of Baal and the 400 prophets of the Asherah to a demonstration of power: their gods against the power of the Lord.

These 850 men were the false prophets, the satanic priests '... *who ate at Jezebel's table*' (1 Kings 18:19). They were the most powerful, demonized individuals that the hosts of darkness could produce. King Ahab, Jezebel's husband, sent a message out to 'all the sons of Israel', and the nation came to witness the conflict between the God of Elijah and the demigods of Jezebel.

The terms of the challenge were simple: each was to place an ox upon an altar. Elijah then said,

> '... *you call upon the name of your god, and I will call on the name of the Lord, and the God who answers by fire, He is God.*'

Six hours later the cult priests still could produce no fire; twelve hours passed and Elijah began to mock them,

> '*Call out with a loud voice, for he is a god; either he is occupied or gone aside ... perhaps he is asleep and needs to be awakened.*'

Just before evening, Elijah prayed over his sacrifice and,

> '*The fire of the Lord fell, and consumed the burnt offering ... and when all the people saw it, they fell on their faces; and they said, "The Lord, He is God; the Lord, He is God."*'   (2 Kings 18:16–40)

Immediately after this powerful witness of the Lord, Elijah had the Hebrews hold the prophets of Baal and all of them were put to death.

We would suppose that, at this point, Elijah would have gone into Jezreel and asked God to finish off Jezebel, but he did not. In fact – and this may surprise you – Elijah came under spiritual warfare. Jezebel, in a fit of rage, released a flood of witchcraft and demonic power against Elijah that put fear into his heart. Elijah ran. You may ask, 'How could such a mighty prophet turn and run?' The answer is not simple. In fact, the situation worsened. We then see Elijah sitting under a juniper tree, bewailing that he is no better than his fathers – actually praying that he might die! (1 Kings 19:4). What pressure overwhelmed this great man of God that he would fall prey to fear and discouragement? The spirit of Jezebel.

And now, let the reader understand. **When you war against the principality of Jezebel, even though you stand against her lusts and witchcrafts, you must guard against the power-demons of Fear and Discouragement, for these she will send against you to distract you from your warfare and your victory!**

The Drama Continues ...

It is an established principle in the spirit realm that one can impart a measure of the spirit-side of himself to another without the fullness of his own spirit diminishing. We see this when Moses' spirit was placed upon the seventy elders (Numbers 11:24–25). We can behold this in the process of the *'father's sins'* being *'passed on to the children.'* And, of course, we see this in Christ's Spirit dwelling within us. With this concept in mind, we can understand how the spirit of Elijah was sent to minister through the soul of John the Baptist.

Once before, Elijah's spirit had been placed upon another individual. You will remember that Elisha, the prophet who succeeded Elijah, received a double portion of Elijah's spirit (2 Kings 2:9–10). Now, again, the spirit of Elijah was ministering, activating, inspiring and creating in John the Baptist that same kind of intensity which dwelt in Elijah himself. John was to go, *'... as a forerunner before the Lord in the spirit and power of Elijah...'* (Luke 1:15–17). Jesus said of the Baptist, *... he himself is Elijah, who* *was to come'* (Matthew 11:14; 17:11–13). John even **looked** like Elijah. He had returned: the spirit of Elijah was commissioned and sent into the world.

Like Elijah, John proclaimed the need for repentance wherever he saw sin. One such area was in the adulterous lives of King Herod and his wife, Herodias. When John confronted them, Herodias had him imprisoned (Mark 6:19). But who was this manipulating and controlling in the dark, spiritual side of Herodias? As Elijah's spirit ministered through John, so **Jezebel** had surfaced into this world through Herodias.

What Jezebel did to Elijah in the wilderness, Herodias now did to John; Jezebel hurled **fear** and **discouragement**, which leads to self-doubt and confusion, against the servant of God. John the Baptist, who had visibly seen the Spirit descend as a dove upon Christ, who heard God's audible voice bearing witness that Jesus was the Son of God, was now asking if Jesus truly was the Messiah, or should they look for another (Matthew 11:3).

> *'And a strategic day came when Herod ... gave a banquet.'*
> (Mark 6:21)

'Strategic' is the perfect word to describe the timing of this event. For in this war between the spirits of Elijah and Jezebel, Herodias had her daughter dance before Herod, enticing out of him a promise to give whatever she asked. At her mother's request – more truly, at **Jezebel's** request – she demanded the head of the Baptist. And temporarily, the confrontation between the spirits of these two eternal enemies subsided.

Elijah Is Coming!

Two thousand years ago, Jesus stated that the ministry of Elijah was not over. He promised,

> *'Elijah is coming and will restore all things...'*
>
> (Matthew 17:11)

Malachi the prophet also wrote,

> *'Behold, I am going to send you Elijah the prophet before the coming of the great and terrible day of the Lord and he will restore.'*   (Malachi 4:5–6)

Elijah *is* coming to war and restore! He came before the Great Day and he is returning before the Terrible Day of the Lord!

Remember, however, the principle of spirit mentioned earlier, that one can impart a measure of the spirit-side of himself to another without the fullness of his own spirit diminishing. **For today, even as God did with Elijah, Elisha and John the Baptist, the Lord is raising up an Elijah company of prophets, Spirit-filled men and women sent forth to prepare the way for the return of Christ!**

Let it also be known that, if Elijah is coming before Jesus returns, so also is Jezebel. Indeed, do you not see her in our land in the abundance of witchcraft and harlotries? Do you not hear her brazen voice rejecting God's authority and exalting her rebellion in feminism? Have you not beheld her causing even God's *'bondservants'* to *'commit acts of immorality?'* (Revelation 2:20). Seeing Jezebel so blatantly manifest herself only confirms that the spirit of Elijah is also here bringing repentance and raising up warring prophets throughout our land! In fact, if you are going to serve God during the reign of a 'Jezebel', the warfare itself will thrust you into a prophetic anointing simply that you may survive!

In the Old Testament we see how God destroyed Jezebel. Jehu, the newly crowned king of Israel, was sent by the word of the Lord through Elijah's successor, Elisha, to fulfil God's promise. As Jehu and his men furiously drove their chariots toward Jezreel, the kings of Israel and Judah came out to meet him,

> *"'Is it peace Jehu?" they asked. And he answered,*
> *"What peace, so long as the harlotries of your mother*
> *Jezebel and her witchcrafts are so many?"'*
>
> (2 Kings 9:21–26)

And Jehu slew the two kings. Immediately afterward, he rode into Jezreel to confront Jezebel. The Word tells us that when she saw him, she painted her eyes and adorned her head, and looking out an upper window, she called to him,

> *"'Is it well Zimri (Jehu), your master's murderer?"*
> *Then he lifted up his face to the window and said,*
> *"Who is on my side? Who?" And two or three*
> *eunuchs looked down at him.*
> *And he said, "Throw her down." So they threw her*
> *down, and some of her blood was sprinkled on the wall*
> *and on the horses, and he trampled her under foot.'*
>
> (2 Kings 9:30–33 NAS/KJ)

There was something in Jehu's spirit that we must possess today in our war against Jezebel. While we must be compassionate toward those captured by Jezebel, Jehu had no mercy, no hope for reform, no compromise or sympathy whatsoever toward this demonic spirit! Jehu '*... trampled her under foot.*' While she lay bleeding and near death, he finished her beneath the feet of his horse!

So also with us, we must have no tolerance whatsoever for this spirit! **There can be no peace, no relaxing under our 'fig tree', until Jezebel is slain!** We must stop living for comfort as long as her harlotries and witchcrafts are so many in our land! We must refuse to settle for a false peace based on compromise and fear, especially when the Spirit of God is calling for 'War!'

It is significant that the **eunuchs** cast her down. Some of you who are reading this have been made eunuchs, slaves to this evil spirit. Today, right now, God is giving you the privilege of participating in the eternal judgment against

Jezebel. **You** cast her down! Side with God, and let the judgments of God come forth!

It is time for the prophets to unite against this spirit! Under the anointing of Elijah, in the power of the Holy Spirit, let us arise in the indignation of Jehu and cast Jezebel down!

Even now, we wash ourselves in the Precious Blood, and having been cleansed from any defilement of sin, we bind and plunder the stronghold of Jezebel!

Pray with us:

> *'Spirit of Jezebel, in the authority of Jesus Christ, which He gives us as His servants, we release your captives! We set free your slaves! We speak to the eunuchs, cast down your sympathetic strongholds toward Jezebel! Cast down her evil imaginations from your minds! In the power of Jesus' name, we release you from her psychic grip upon your soul. In the authority of the Living Christ, we proclaim HOLY WAR upon the spirit of Jezebel! Amen.'*

Chapter 19

Our Experience with Jezebel

What we present to you comes from our experience. We offer you no theories, no speculations. What we share with you has worked.

To Deliver, We Ourselves Must Be Delivered

'He will deliver one who is not innocent, and he will be delivered through the cleanness of your hands.'

(Job 22:30)

There is a difference between repenting for a sin and actually pulling down the stronghold within us that produced the sin. The first involves faith in the cross of Christ; the second demands we embrace crucifixion ourselves. In this regard, in 1971 the Lord began a foundational work of cleansing my heart from the influence of the Jezebel spirit.

This season of repentance lasted about forty days. During that time, through the Holy Spirit, the stronghold which was tolerant toward the spirit of Jezebel was pulled down. I should make it clear that I was not repenting again for sins previously washed and forgiven. As was stated earlier, my repentance was not for sin, but for the **nature** that caused my sins. This is the essence of pulling down strongholds: we destroy the defiling, oppressive **system of thinking** which, through the years, has been built into our nature. My goal was simply that I be renewed in '... *the spirit of* [my] *mind'* (Ephesians 4:23).

The manner in which this happened was as follows: The Holy Spirit brought to mind many of the sins from my unsaved youth. Two or three times a day, every day, in dreams or as I worked, the Lord brought events to my mind. As the Lord revealed these incidents, I covered each memory with the blood of Jesus. Each time I prayed I knew that, through the Spirit, another 'stone' was being removed from this fortress in my mind.

Finally, the Lord revealed, through a dream, that this stronghold had been pulled down. In the dream two men were talking, one of whom was holding a baby. The one holding the child used a vile word in his conversation. Suddenly embarrassed because of the infant, he quickly reassured himself that the baby was so innocent that it did not know the meaning of the word. In the dream, I realized that I also did not know the meaning of this word and, in this, the grace of God had brought a new innocence into my heart of which the baby in the dream was a symbol. At that time, I knew nothing of the spirit of Jezebel. Nevertheless, the Lord was building in me a measure of immunity against it.

Our First Encounter With Jezebel

During the 1970s I pastored in an organization which had scores of men who functioned in the revelation gifts of wisdom and knowledge. There was 'day and night' prayer, beautiful worship, commitment and power. As the Lord was to Jacob on the plains of Moab, so He was also to us like the horns of the wild ox (Numbers 22–25). There seemed no curse or omen that worked against us; God had given us His blessing, success seemed inevitable. But as Balaam counselled Balak to seduce the Israelites with the daughters of Moab, so the spirit of Jezebel launched its attack upon this work of God.

If the enemy cannot attack you directly, he will seek to

bring you into sin, thereby positioning you under the judgments of God. When the Jezebel spirit began to manifest itself, and tolerance toward sexual sins increased, I approached the founder of the movement with my concerns. Meeting with him privately, I entreated him as a son does a father; but he dismissed me. Three months later I approached him again, appealing this time to the entire governmental team which was with him, warning them with tears that the judgment of the Lord against tolerating Jezebel was sickness and death (Revelation 2:22–23). Once more I was dismissed. Several months later I was removed from leadership, and then, ultimately, forced from the group. Within months after I left the leader divorced his wife, and less than a year later he married his secretary. Within two years he was dead from prostate cancer.

The impact of this experience was both devastating and enlightening. Even though I personally went through a period of great discouragement and self-doubt, I learned much about Jezebel and the sin of presumption. I saw that when men assume God will not judge them, it is only a matter of time before the tempter comes to destroy them. It is significant that, while Jesus had the spirits of wisdom and understanding, counsel, strength and knowledge, His **delight** was *'in the fear of the Lord'* (Isaiah 11:2–3). The sin of presumption is the antithesis of the fear of the Lord. It is the harbinger of future defeat.

Releasing Souls Through Prayer

That was our first experience with the spirit of Jezebel, though not the last. In 1985, during a time of counselling, we discerned that this spirit was the controlling influence, directing the lesser demons of homosexuality and lesbianism. The Lord instructed us to war against Jezebel and in one month's time three people were delivered from these perversions! The next month the local cable network removed the Playboy Channel. People began calling for help with sexual problems and needing deliverance from fantasies. Even pastors and their wives, without knowing we were doing warfare, were calling to confess sins and receive deliverance. By focusing our warfare against this Jezebel, many in her grip were being set free!

At the same time, the warfare increased considerably against both my family and our church. A demon named 'Fault-Finder' (which we had not discerned until months later) brought division and conflict into the congregation. Certain people, whom we loved deeply, suddenly were turned against us with unexplained hatred. Suspicion mounted in the church and a time of de-stabilization occurred. Nevertheless, we continued warring against this spirit, convinced our warfare was effective.

One night, however, the spirit of Jezebel appeared at the foot of our bed. I felt paralyzed, unable to speak or even cry for help. This spirit, which had alienated even close friends, was now standing before me, unfiltered by a human body. All my natural life seemed literally drained from my body. I felt that only Christ's life sustained me.

No audible words were spoken, but through thought-transference, this principality put the following words into my mind, 'Continue to pray as you are and I will kill you and the members of your church.' The spirit faded, but even after it had apparently left, I was barely able to move. My mind was a quagmire of discouraging thoughts: 'Why should I pray for these people? Why suffer when, on any given day, I don't know who will be turned against me?' Eventually, the Holy Spirit intervened and the oppression broke.

But Jezebel's death-threat was not idle. Less than a week later, a woman in the church called asking for help. Her husband had taken drugs and was threatening her and her children. We made provisions for her and she and her youngsters escaped. At 1.00 am that same night I received a phone call from her enraged husband. This man, a self-styled Nazi and owner of thirty-four guns, was demanding I tell him where his wife was. He said, 'If you don't tell me where my wife is, **"I will kill you and the members of your**

church!"' These were the exact words the spirit of Jezebel had used in my bedroom less than one week earlier! It was obvious that the Jezebel spirit had found and raised up a vessel to carry out the death threat of the previous week.

It is not normal practice for pastors to pray **for** a snow-storm on a Saturday night, but we prayed that night and the light snow falling outside turned into a blizzard, dropping ten inches of snow by church time Sunday morning. Those of us at church prayed again and bound Jezebel from the man who had threatened us. Eventually, to God's glory, this individual accepted the Lord as his Saviour.

This has been a summary of our experience with the spirit of Jezebel. If you witness to the reality of our message, then pray about your involvement in fighting this principality. What we have written is not based upon theory or conjecture, but experience. Our testimony in this warfare is simply this: the Lord Jesus Himself has given us His authority *'over **all** the power of the enemy...'* His promise is faithful:

'...and nothing shall injure you.'   (Luke 10:19)

Chapter 20

Strategy Against the Spirit of Jezebel

You cannot defeat the enemy simply with prayer. To topple Satan's empire we must be transformed into Christ's likeness.

Our War Against Jezebel

The church that successfully wars against Jezebel will be a church that inherits the glorious *'morning star'*, which will be a visible outward glory, a symbol of hidden, inward purity. It will be a church that exercises *'authority over the nations'*, uniquely because it has conquered the Jezebel spirit which sought to strip God's servants of authority. It will be a church in which the gift of healing is an integral part of their body ministry (Revelation 2:26–28).

There are great prizes to winning the war against Jezebel. Although every victory is initiated by prayer, the rewards of God will not be attained only through intercession. As we have stated, victory begins with the name of Jesus on our lips. But it is not consummated until the nature of Jesus is in our heart.

Therefore, in regard to our war against Jezebel, we must allow the Holy Spirit to expose where we are tolerant and sympathetic to its ways. **We cannot be successful in the heavenly war if we are not victorious in the battlefield of our minds.** There is only one realm of final victory against the enemy: Christlikeness.

Jesus is He '... *Who searches the hearts and the minds*' (Revelation 2:23). Our victory in every battle begins here, in our '*hearts and minds*'. Consequently, we cannot tolerate Jezebelian thinking in any area. Our concept of church must expand beyond buildings into a way of life we practice everywhere. Since **we** are the church, let us realize that we are still in the church when we are home. When we turn on television to an immoral program, we are still in the church, tolerating the spirit of Jezebel.

If a husband is afraid of his strong-willed wife or unable to serve as the head of his household, although he is not in the worship building, he is still in the church tolerating Jezebel. Our time spent in the worship service is necessary, but it is a very small part of our continuing church-life. It is in the routine things of daily living where the strongholds of Jezebel must be confronted and destroyed.

It Takes an 'Ahab' to Tolerate Jezebel

There is a spirit which works with Jezebel. The effect of this demon is that it floods the soul of a man with weakness and fear. Its name is Ahab; his nature is 'one who **gives** his authority to Jezebel.'

The Ahab spirit occupies the areas of tolerance within a man's mind. The man feels almost drugged in his struggle against Jezebel. To win against Jezebel, one must conquer the nature of Ahab.

The man who is married to a domineering wife will exhibit one of two responses: he will either be fearful in other relationships in his life; or he will tend to resent women in general. If he is an employer, he will be overly harsh, control-oriented toward females, quick to put them 'in their place'. This is a manifestation of his resentment toward his wife.

The essence of Ahab is a title, 'husband', and a position, 'head', but the man has no real authority. When Ahab was king, Jezebel ruled. The man who cannot govern his house-hold in godly, protective authority will not exercise his spiritual authority elsewhere. Such a man needs to repent of his fears and firmly, with gentleness, set his home in order.

But let us further clarify authority. Authority is simply delegated responsibility. The emphasis is not on being the boss, but being responsible. The substructure upon which divine authority comes forth is divine love. Headship in the home is simply the man taking loving responsibility for the condition of his family. No man will have peace in his home if he views authority as simply the domination of his wife. God would have couples making decisions together, each drawing upon the wisdom of the other, enjoying themselves as friends in open and loving communion. God's answer to dealing with Jezebel is not to exchange one form of oppression (Jezebel's), for another (the man's). Our objective is to replace Jezebel's concept of security with the security a woman receives when she is tenderly loved by her husband. Thus, the man wins the war against Jezebel by becoming Christlike.

The woman overcomes the haughtiness of Jezebel by seeking the meekness of Christ. She pursues a *'quiet and gentle spirit'* (1 Peter 2:23–3:2), which is natural to Christlikeness. The woman must see God's wisdom in the divine order of the family and honour her husband as her head. If she is unmarried, she should be submitted to the order God has established in her church as unto the Lord. Her humility and peace in serving others is a sign of destruction to the nature of Jezebel (Philippians 1:28).

The woman conquers the sensual side of Jezebel by renouncing her feminine charms, which *'are deceitful'* (Proverbs 31:30a), and her *'many persuasions'* (Proverbs 7:21), which are enticing. She refuses the sensual look of the eyes and seductive softening of the voice. If she is married, her beauty is given to her husband. If she is single, she adorns her inner person with the spiritual qualities of the fruit of the Spirit, knowing that if she compromises her standards with God, she will inevitably find a man who will compromise his standards with her. The true man God has for her is a godly man in search of a virtuous woman. Her victory begins with prayer, but it is consummated by transformation.

What we become in Christ, **as His people**, must be the exact opposite of the spirit of Jezebel. Is she rebellious? We must become submissive. Is she proud and haughty? We must become meek and lowly of heart. Is she a control demon? We must be gentle and willing to yield. Does Jezebel send forth witchcraft and immorality, fear and discouragement? We must live a crucified life in the purity of Christ, full of love and faith for our vision. Again, it is Who Christ becomes in us that establishes our victory against the spirit of Jezebel.

Corporate Warfare Against Satan's Powers

'And they lifted their voice to God with one accord.'
(Acts 4:24)

As important as it is to win the war against Jezebel in the home, we must also join together for corporate prayer and warfare. Corporate prayer is the united intercession of the church against the powers of darkness.* This type of warfare can be accomplished with a great variety of expression and with a minimum of requirements. Nevertheless, those requirements are essential to effective warfare.

1. Worship should be part of warfare
With great variety, worship and praise should be integrated into warfare. During our warfare, various individuals spontaneously will lead out with appropriate songs. Keep your eyes on Jesus and stay thankful!

---

* An audio tape, demonstrating a typical time of warfare is available upon request. Send $4.50 to Advancing Church Ministries, PO Box 10102, Cedar Rapids IA 52410

2. Intercession should be Spirit led

This is more than 'praying in tongues'. It requires we learn to listen. Often, corporate prayer is actually hindered by someone dominating the group with loud, insensitive 'tongues'. When you pray corporately, there is a **common fountain** from which those who pray must draw. It requires we be responsive to the subtle changes of the Spirit, as He guides the group into creative agreement. As individuals we seek to keep our prayers short (two to five minutes); we address one need at a time, leaving the door open for others to pray in agreement.

3. Seek to remain consistent to scheduled prayer times

This may sound like we are seeking to control the Holy Spirit, but the more predictable the schedule, the more people can commit themselves to it. However, stay open for those special seasons when the Lord orders additional intercession.

4. Do not become presumptuous

In fact, if someone resorts to calling the devil names, 'daring him to fight', etc., instruct him that he is out of order. In prayer, use the Word, the Spirit and the Name of Jesus; anything more than these is fleshly.

5. Keep all talk to a minimum

Save all but essential conversation for after prayer.

6. Those who engage in warfare should be trained and approved by church leadership

Every church should have a 'warfare team' as well as a 'backup team' which prays for those on the front lines. The backup team should consist of those in training or those who feel called only to pray.

Chapter 21

God Will Judge Your Judgment

The spirit of Babylon is the spirit of compromise with the world. Wherever there is compromise in our hearts with the devil, that compromise places us on the back of a beast that ultimately seeks our destruction!

Identifying the Spirit of Babylon

The spirit of Babylon has been in the earth since civilization began. It is essential to understand this spirit if we desire to walk in God's Kingdom without compromise, for the spirit of Babylon epitomizes self-exaltation, and self-exaltation is the source of compromise.

Originally, Babylon was more than a wealthy, glamorous city; it was primarily a **religious** city. To understand this gives us great insight into the nature of this enemy. Genesis 11:4 tells us that the common intent of its people was to build for themselves a city, '*... and a tower whose top will reach into heaven.*' More than their advanced skills in art and warfare, their pride was in their religion. When the Lord confused their tongues and scattered them across the earth, the spirit of Babylon spread throughout the world, and the desire to '*reach into heaven*' through man-made religions proliferated in every nation.

We also see in this spirit the ambition '*to make for ourselves a name*'. So much has this influence become a part of our human nature that Solomon observed,

> '...every labor and every skill which is done is the
> result of rivalry between a man and his neighbor.'
>
> (Ecclesiastes 4:4)

Rivalry and the desire to make for oneself a name still comprise the nature of the spirit of Babylon.

One last thing about the origins of Babylon: the Scripture says the people journeyed east to the land of Shinar and 'settled there' (Genesis 11:2). Anytime a church stops pressing on and begins to 'settle down', expect something Babylonian in nature to arise.

The influence of Babylonian philosophy is also seen in the Book of Daniel. You will remember it was Babylon that conquered the Hebrews and carried them off into captivity. There Daniel was raised up to sit with the Chaldean wise men and conjurers who counselled King Nebuchadnezzar. We see this spirit in the thinking of the Babylonian priests when they were required to know what only the Almighty knew. They said,

> 'The thing which the king demands is difficult, and there
> is no one else who could declare it to the king except
> gods, whose dwelling place is not with mortal flesh.'
>
> (Daniel 2:11)

We can recognize the influence of Babylon in any people or church that offer lip service to a God far off, a deity whose dwelling place is not with men. In contrast, Jesus is our Emmanuel, *'God with us!'* The very essence of true Christianity is Christ in us, the hope of glory. You can discern the spirit of Babylon in a church that honours God in heaven without having any relationship with Him on earth.

Babylon Will Be Destroyed

The spirit of Babylon is all around us, both in our society in general and in the Christian church in particular. In the Book of Revelation we see those who have compromised with this spirit. They are seen as '...*a woman sitting on a scarlet beast*' (Revelation 17:3). Upon her forehead a name was written, *'Babylon the Great, the mother of harlots.'* (Revelation 17:5).

To discern the spirit of Babylon, look first for pride: *'Let us make for ourselves a name.'* Then, look for worldliness: *'the woman was clothed in purple and scarlet, and adorned with gold and precious stones and pearls...'* Finally, where people are drunk with lusts for pleasure, you will see: *'in her hand a gold cup full of abominations and of the unclean things of her immorality'* (Revelation 17:4).

The command of God is,

> *'Come out of her, My people, that you may not partici-*
> *pate in her sins, and that you may not receive of her*
> *plagues.'*   (Revelation 18:4)

When we are called out of Babylon, it is a call into Christlikeness. In this hour God is certainly calling the church to enter into meekness, moderation and purity of heart. The Holy Spirit has been judging and cleansing the Babylonian strongholds from the church. Indeed, the sins of Babylon will soon be fulfilled by plagues, which even now are falling upon her. In His mercy, God calls us out of this evil.

The Revelation of John continues,

> *'The beast ... will hate the harlot and will make her*
> *desolate and naked, and will eat her flesh and will burn*
> *her up with fire.'*   (Revelation 17:16)

Anytime we decide to coexist with the devil, it leaves us desolate and naked, suffering in unquenchable fire. This warning must be heard by each of us as individuals. In the sanctuary of our hearts, we must decide we are not going to compromise with Babylon in any way.

Those Who Conquer

At the same time, the Apocalypse speaks of a people who not only came out of Babylon, but they rose up as an army against it. Under the Lord's direction, they became instrumental in God's judgment of her. Concerning the fall of Babylon, Revelation 18:20 reads, literally,

> *'Rejoice over her, O heaven, and you saints and apostles and prophets, because God has judged your judgment of her.'*

John wrote here of saints, apostles and prophets in the last days whose words and whose purity became a source of judgment upon the spirit of Babylon! In fact, God will judge **their** judgment!

The Lord Jesus not only wants us separate from this spirit, but to be warring against it. In other words, as we agree in spirit and character, in word and behaviour, with the Word of God concerning righteousness, God will put in our mouths His judgments concerning evil! The simplicity and purity of our lives will be instrumental in binding the powers of Babylon and releasing her prisoners!

We are not fighting flesh and blood, but the powers of darkness that hold people captive. *'Through the church'* the manifold wisdom of God is made known ... *unto the principalities and powers, the rulers in the heavenly places'* (Ephesians 3:10 KJ). Before Jesus returns, His church will be brought up to His standard in all aspects (Ephesians 4:11–15). And that includes becoming an army that hates wickedness and loves righteousness, an army that, as it follows Christ, **initiates** spiritual warfare against the various gates of hell.

Jesus: Our Warrior King

Jesus is not returning as the 'meek and mild' Lamb Whom the world crucified. No, He is not coming again to be humiliated. He is returning

> *'to be glorified in His saints ... and to be marveled at by those who have believed.'*   (2 Thessalonians 1:10)

Within His saints first, He shall establish His rule in glory and be revealed in power (Revelation 2:26; Jude 14:15). He is returning as the King of kings and the Lord of lords. This Lamb returns to earth treading *'...the wine press of the fierce wrath of God!'* (Revelation 19:15).

Speaking through the prophet, the Holy Spirit says,

> *'The Lord will go forth like a warrior, He will arouse His zeal like a man of war. He will utter a shout, yes, He will raise a war cry. He will prevail against His enemies.'*   (Isaiah 42:13)

Do you hear the war cry our King is raising? It is the call to put away the idols of Babylon and approach the hour of our destiny with zeal and willing obedience to Jesus. As it is written,

> *'Thy people will volunteer freely in the day of Thy power!'*   (Psalm 110:3)

Especially as we approach the end of this age, it is essential we understand that God's purpose is to conform us to the image of His Son. We are to grow up *'in all aspects'* of the Holy One, even He who is the Captain of the Hosts!

As you enter into the administration of the victory of Jesus Christ, what was once a walk filled with blindness and darkness will now become a walk of vision and light. Your words will declare God's purpose, and His purpose will empower your words. You will rejoice as you see the Spirit of God *'judge **your** judgment'* of Babylon.

> 'Heavenly Father, we worship You. We declare that Your name shall be exalted in all the earth, even the name You gave Your Son, Jesus! We renounce seeking to make names for ourselves, we cast off the illusions of the world, we repent of the lusts of comfort and pleasure.

Lord, we judge the spirit of Babylon! We release Your people from its drunkenness and immoralities! We line our lives up according to the standard of Your righteous judgments, that you might judge our judgment of this spirit. In Jesus' name. Amen!'

Chapter 22

Discerning the Nature of the Enemy

The Lord is uniting His people, raising up an army, equipping them and preparing them to take their cities.

Hitting the Heart of Your Adversary

In the realm of spirit the **name** of an entity always corresponds to its **nature**. You will notice that there are many names given to the Lord in Scripture. Yet, each revealed name was actually a deeper revelation of His nature (Genesis 22:14; Exodus 3:14). Similarly, the names of the Lord's angels are also self-descriptive.

This principle of consistency between the name and nature of spiritual beings holds true in discerning the activity and purpose of evil spirits. To defeat the rulers of darkness we must know their nature – what to expect, what their tactics are and how they apply those tactics against our weaknesses.

In the Bible, the term 'unclean spirit' is a generic term used simply to draw a distinction between angelic spirits and evil spirits. But if you want to bring deliverance, you need to know the **nature** of a specific unclean spirit; that is, whether the unclean spirit is a spirit of fear or sexual lust, etc. You do not need to ask it any more questions once you know its nature.

Consider that the name of the unclean spirit inhabiting the Gerasene demoniac was *'Legion...'* Why? ...*for we are many'* (Mark 5:6–9). Knowing the name helped Jesus discern its nature, thus facilitating the actual deliverance. When John describes the fallen angel in Revelation 9:11 as the 'king' over the demons in the bottomless pit, he reveals this ruler's name in Hebrew as, *'Abaddon, and in the Greek he has the name Apollyon.'* In English, these names are 'Destruction' and 'Destroyer' respectively. Again, the name and nature match.

Once you know its nature, however, you do not need to know its name. If you were in warfare against 'Abaddon', you could identify the spirit with the name 'Destruction' or 'Destroyer' as readily as using the Hebrew name, 'Abaddon'. Or, you could war against it, if God so led you, by simply calling it the spirit of destruction. How do we defeat the enemy? Victory begins with the name of Jesus on our lips; it is consummated by the nature of Jesus in our hearts.

Follow the Lamb!

We have touched on a few of the enemies of God in this book. It is very important to **not** charge ahead, attacking principalities in warfare without having strategies and without people praying for the protection of those doing warfare.

In Scripture, we have a clear picture of the proper balance in all warfare:

> '...*the armies which are in heaven ... were following Him.'* (Revelation 19:11–16)

In no other dimension of life will we find the phrase, 'a little knowledge is a dangerous thing', more true than in spiritual warfare. The armies which are in heaven **follow!** Who do they follow? **Jesus!**

Therefore, let us be very conscious and very careful to be followers of the Lord. From our experiences, it is vital that the people in your church be trained in warfare **before** laying a large-scale siege against the enemy. Your attack against the strongholds of hell will be in the areas of your knowledge. Satan, on the other hand, will counter-attack in the areas of your ignorance.

It is essential we understand the difference between being taught and being **trained**. Reading this book is being taught, being personally led by the Lord Jesus is being trained. David wrote,

> '*He **trains** my hands for battle, so that my arms can bend a bow of bronze.*' (Psalm 18:34)

This book is meant to inform you of your need for training and to provide certain insights and guidelines. What you will learn in confrontational warfare and obeying the Lord on the actual battleground, will far exceed that which any book teaching will provide. Your confidence must be securely in the Lord, not in this book.

The Lord Is Raising Up His Army!

There are a growing number of churches around the world who are being gathered together by the Lord for war. Currently, many are seeking God for strategies and wisdom concerning their region of ministry. Together, we will believe the Lord for those anointed men and women who, united in the Spirit of Jesus Christ, '*will put ten thousand to flight*' (Leviticus 26:7–8).

A Last Word ...

As we embrace God's eternal plan, which is to make us in the image of Christ, let us remember that no weapon formed against us shall prosper, and every tongue that accuses us in judgment we will condemn (Isaiah 54:17). As we capture every thought unto the obedience of Christ, know with certainty, there are those who have gone before us who, even now, are ready to punish all disobedience when our obedience is made complete (2 Corinthians 10:1–6; Jude 14–16; Mark 4:29).

Be assured, our weapons are mighty as we pray in the power of Christ's might! (Ephesians 6:19) Be confident and bold – for our prayers, like arrows, are in the heart of the King's enemies! (Psalm 45:5). Jesus Himself has gone before us; the fear of Him has the enemies' camp in disarray!

To those of you who are of the nature of Gideon, the Lord says, 'Shrink not from your call, though you consider yourself but a weak, foolish or base thing, for I have chosen to use you to nullify the things that are. (1 Corinthians 1:28). Rejoice and be exceedingly glad, for I Myself have purposed to consummate the battle by revelation of My fullness in your life! I was watching Satan fall from heaven like lightning. Remember, I have given you authority to tread upon serpents and scorpions, and over all the power of the enemy, and nothing shall injure you!' (Luke 10:18–19).

A Short Glossary

'For we wrestle not against flesh and blood, but against principalities, against powers, against the rulers of the darkness of this world, against spiritual wickedness in high places.'
(Ephesians 6:12 KJ)

Heavenly places (Ephesians 6:12; 3:10). When the Scriptures refer to 'heaven', they may be speaking of any of three places which the context of the reference interprets. The first heaven is the atmospheric heaven, the sky (Psalm 19:1). The third heaven is the most familiar definition of heaven: first of many levels of glory, which are crowned by the highest of Heavens, the dwelling place of the Father God (Matthew 6:9).

The heaven which is the unique object of this study is the spirit realm which immediately surrounds the consciousness of mankind. It is this realm, known frequently in the Scriptures as the 'heavenly places', which is the battleground of our spiritual warfare. Within this realm, good and evil spirits clash in the battle for men's souls. Ultimately, when the Lord Jesus returns and all evil is banished, this heaven will be filled with the glory of God.

Demons, Devils. (Greek: *Daimon*, demons.) King James wrongly translates 'demons' as 'devils'. There is only one devil, Satan, but there are many demons. Demons were once angels *'who left their first estate'* (Jude 6). Demons are fallen angels (Revelations 12:9; Matthew 25:41).

There are two separate words translated 'devil' in the New Testament, each representing a different spiritual entity. Demons differ in degrees of wickedness (Matthew 12:45). Everything from fairies and imps to principalities and powers can be categorized as demons when the term 'demon' is used as a generic term. However, when 'demon' is used as a specific term, it usually is a reference to any number of unclean spirits, such as deaf and dumb spirits, as well as spirits which masquerade as human thoughts.

Demons are the ground troops of hell. They are the most abundant of evil spirits and, evidently, God has given a legal right to demons to occupy any territory that exists in defiant rebellion to His will, including mankind. Jude 6 tells that these fallen angels are kept in eternal bonds of darkness. Darkness is not merely a lightless region, but a spiritual place of moral depravity. The responsibility to *'cast out demons'* belongs to all believers (Mark 16:17).

(Greek: *'Diabolos'*, an accuser, a slanderer.) One of the names of Satan. From this word the English word 'devil' is derived, and should be applied only to Satan *Vines Expository Dictionary*. (See 'Satan', below.)

Principality (Ephesians 3:10; 6:12). (Greek: *'Arche'*.) The word means 'beginning, government, rule' and is used to describe a class of spirit-beings in the satanic hierarchy. Principalities rule over 'Powers' as well as the more numerous subcategories of demons. Principalities influence countries, regions within countries, states, cities and even churches. These are Governmental spirits in the system of hell and are the spiritual counterpart of 'archangels' in Heaven. They issue assignments and direct local warfare against the church. In general, they are the 'administrators of evil' throughout any given area.

The means through which the church successfully wars against Principalities is through Christ's spiritual authority and the principle of displacement. Principalities are not 'cast out', for they do not dwell in people, they dwell in 'heavenly places'. They are displaced in the spirit-realm by the ascendancy of Christ in the church and, through the church, into the community.

Powers (Matthew 24:29; Ephesians 3:10; 6:12.) Working with Principalities, but in subjection to them, are what the Bible calls 'Powers'. The energy of a Power is beamed outward from itself, broadcast like radio waves, over the territory. A Power is a major demonic spirit whose primary activity is to blanket a given area with the energy of its particular evil. They are called 'Powers' because that is what they are: **powers** of darkness. They are the evil counterparts of the angelic class, Virtues. A church may have a particular Virtue ministering through it, such as Joy or Faith, the same way a Power of Fear or Depression may minister through a certain degenerate section of town.

Many people during any particular week will struggle with the same unique problem. The source of this activity is often a particular Power influencing an area. Instead of dealing directly with each person, binding the Power over the area and then covering the people, spiritually, with the blood of Jesus causes the intensity of their battle to subside and victory to come.

Powers occupy a jurisdiction that is usually county-wide,

although a Power may frequent the mind of an influential person or build a certain negative attitude within a church. Major Powers also influence the spirit realm over entire regions of countries. Different Powers will work together under the control of a Principality, but usually one or two will be the most influential, eventually affecting even the mannerisms of speech in that area. (Compare the hard dialect of the states surrounding New York City with the slower, almost dallying language of sectors in the South.)

As is the case with Principalities, the means through which the church successfully wars against Powers is through the administration of Christ's spiritual authority and the principle of displacement. Powers are not 'cast out', they are **displaced** in the spirit-realm by the fullness of the reign of Christ in the church, and through the intercessory warfare of the saints in the region.

World rulers of darkness (Ephesians 3:10; 6:12). When the Bible speaks of the *'world rulers of darkness'*, it is speaking with reference to a certain class of Principalities, a spiritual entity that, on a national scale, governs other Principalities, as well as the Powers under them. The scope of a World Ruler's influence is world-wide.

In the Book of Daniel, one such Principality was known as the *'prince over Persia'*. This particular World Ruler fought with the angel that was sent in answer to prayer. On the natural level, Cyrus was king of Persia, but in the spirit realm there was another ruler as well. Daniel's intercession, you will remember, was instrumental in obtaining from King Cyrus permission for the Jews to return and rebuild Jerusalem. In the spirit realm, however, the World Ruler was resisting. Finally, Michael, who was an Archangel over Israel (equivalent to the class, world ruler), joined the original angel that was sent to Daniel and defeated the enemy. The influence of the World Rulers, as well as the Principalities and Powers, can be observed in the differing temperaments and cultures of the European nations.

Satan. (Greek: *'Satanas'*, adversary, one who resists.) The principle name of the devil. Satan is the slanderer of men to God and of God to men. His assault against humanity is to cause men to sin, thereby invoking the judgment of God against mankind. Our warfare against Satan is successful when we remain pure and invoke the judgment of God against the devil. One of the ministries of the Holy Spirit is to bring God's judgment against the devil (John 16:11).

Satan is the ultimate source of deception and lies, as well as acts of violence. Jesus said of Satan that he was a thief who came to *'steal, kill and destroy'*. Satan is the tempter. He is also the accuser of the brethren. Scripture also calls him the prince of this world and the god of this age. This author believes that Satan himself does not appear and directly attack people in general, but that the devil reserves his assault for the Lord's anointed (Job, Christ, Peter). Scripturally speaking, Satan was rebuked, but not 'cast out' in the manner of dealing with demons. The church successfully wars against Satan by submitting to God, living, speaking and holding fast to the Word of God, knowing the power of Christ's sacrificial blood, and living the crucified life (Revelation 12:10–12).

Kingdom of God (Matthew 5:3, 10; 6:33; Mark 1:14–15; etc). Scripturally speaking, this phrase always refers to the eternal spiritual reality where the rule of God through Christ originates. The expanse of this heavenly kingdom has two primary manifestations: Heaven in eternity, and the **fragrance** of Heaven in the realm of time, which is revealed and entered through Christ. When this author speaks of 'establishing the kingdom', it is in context with the latter definition. It is not our view that the whole earth must be subdued and made subject to Christ before He returns. Rather, we speak of the kingdom of God as that dimension of eternal life which the redeemed inherit through spiritual rebirth and which the obedient discover in the meaning of Christ's words.

Other Writings *by Francis Frangipane*

In the Presence of God, a powerful and penetrating study of the human heart and how God prepares it for His glory.

The House of the Lord, a challenging and inspirational look at the Lord's view of the church and its commission to turn cities toward heaven.

The River of Life, an edited compilation of messages previously published in a newsletter.

Booklets

Exposing the Accuser of the Brethren
Discerning of Spirits
The Jezebel Spirit
A Time to Seek God